CW01433713

THERE ARE PLACES I
REMEMBER

Steven Scragg

THERE ARE PLACES I
REMEMBER

Liverpool FC and the
Miracle of Istanbul

pitch

First published by Pitch Publishing, 2025

1

pitch

Pitch Publishing
9 Donnington Park,
85 Birdham Road,
Chichester, West Sussex,
PO20 7AJ
www.pitchpublishing.co.uk
info@pitchpublishing.co.uk

A CIP catalogue record is available for this book
from the British Library.

ISBN 978 1 83680 176 4

Typesetting and origination by Pitch Publishing

MIX
Paper | Supporting
responsible forestry
FSC
www.fsc.org   FSC™ C016779

Printed and bound on FSC® certified paper in line with
our continuing commitment to ethical business practices,
sustainability and the environment.

Printed and bound in India by Replika Press Pvt. Ltd.

Contents

For Florence and her many wonderful alter egos: Flo, Floda, the Florax, Flo Rida, Pookie and Flod. The world is there for all of you to conquer.

Also, for Diogo. For ever our number 20.

Acknowledgements

DON'T GET me wrong, that trip to Istanbul would have still been wondrous without them, but it never would have hit the same had it been a journey undertaken with anyone else. Big Andy, Sue, Gary, Elvis, Martin, Stevie and Alison, plus their boys. There was Alan and his then young son Greg too, at least when they belatedly did catch up with us. Also Michaela, who didn't make it in person, only in spirit, after being there for most of the 2004/05 season's adventures following Liverpool, unreasonably denied a ticket to Istanbul because she had to hang around Rainford to do her GCSEs instead. Thank you one and all. It was an absolute blast.

As always, my appreciation goes out to my wife Beverley, plus our collection of children: Sam, Elsie, and Florence. They are supportive distractions of the highest order and keep me grounded. Big thanks also go to my dad, who showed me the path to Liverpool Football Club, dragging me along to Anfield for the first time at the age of three, in November 1977, for the European Super Cup second leg and Kevin Keegan's return in the colours of Hamburger SV. A big up also goes to my sister and brother, Alison and David, who always had to navigate their way around the Subbuteo pitches that I would have laid out on the carpet on a daily basis. Then there is the wonderful Hayley Coleman – the first person who ever told me I can put words together in a readable order.

A thank you also goes to Jamie Carragher for allowing me to grill him on his perspectives, especially the ones he has from half-time in the Liverpool dressing room at the Atatürk Olympic Stadium, while Paul Salt's stories from Monte Carlo, Köln, Turin, Istanbul, and his flight home were priceless.

Further appreciation for their recollections go to: George Scott, Jeff Goulding, Paul Moran, Steve Hales, Keith Salmon, Nick Burgess, Chris Thomas, Keith Wagstaff, Ian Ford, Craig Gregson, Phil Roose, Kirsty Watson, Eddie Starrs, John O'Dwyer, Neil Wilkes, Lee Mcloughlin, Rob Storry, Andy Abbott, and Ivan McDouall.

Meanwhile, this book would not have been born at all, had it not been for my involvement with *These Football Times*, and the encouragement given, be that from editor-in-chief and creator Omar Saleem, or a cabal of podcast comrades from where inspiration for a thousand book projects has been dreamed up: Aidan Williams, Stuart Horsfield, Gary Thacker, Dave Bowler, Chris Lepkowski, Dr Peter Watson, Rob Fletcher, and lastly Paul McParlan, a magnificently militant Blue, who certainly won't be reading this particular release.

Big thanks must also go to Jane at Pitch Publishing for her continued support. To Duncan Olner too, for his magnificent work on the cover.

You have all played your part to perfection.

Introduction

IT IS the green buses that stick in the mind; it wasn't that they were particularly special vehicles, it was instead everything to do with how long you were travelling on them, held captive by the driver for what seemed a never-ending journey between Taksim Square in downtown Beyoğlu and the Atatürk Olympic Stadium, which is situated out in the district of Başakşehir.

Of course, we were all sold the concept that the host stadium of the 2005 Champions League Final was in Istanbul, and while it nominally is in terms of Başakşehir being within the wider province of Istanbul, geographically the Atatürk is further away from Taksim Square than Wigan Athletic's DW Stadium is from Anfield.

Yet we didn't realise this as we made our exit from the epicentre of the vibrant Liverpool pre-match party in order to make our way to the stadium, as the warm afternoon began to point itself toward the early onset of an evening that would both captivate and shock not only those in attendance but also a disbelieving watching world.

Taksim Square had been an ocean of red and white all day, a vista that was the stage of a carefree, joyous open-air party, a location that had been allocated to what was a cross-section of Liverpool supporters, not only those old enough to have lived the glories of Rome, Wembley, and Paris between 1977 and 1984, as well as the tragic events of Heysel in 1985, but also to a new generation of whom many had only experienced the more disjointed fluctuations of the club since 1990.

Banners and flags as far as the eye could see, every inch of Taksim Square was a prime position to find yourself in, while the mood was one of exuberance and partial bewilderment. Yes, we very much felt like we belonged to a day like this, but so much of what had unfolded across the previous three years leading up to this moment confounded the fact that we were there, rather than José Mourinho's Chelsea, Fabio Capello's Juventus, or arguably even Klaus Augenthaler's Bayer Leverkusen.

Intrigued locals were drawn into the party by the blizzard of colour, the songs, the carousing, the tree boy who was prime entertainment outside the bars, and the sheer lack of Englishness on display; this was a scene that was a thousand times detached from the warnings that had been sounded for Liverpool's travelling support to look after itself as it strolled into the very same place that had been front and centre when the Leeds United fans Christopher Loftus and Kevin Speight were brutally stabbed to death a little over five years earlier, when there to see their team take on Galatasaray in the first leg of the 1999/2000 UEFA Cup semi-final.

Instead, the warmth of the weather was matched by that of the inhabitants of Istanbul, the vast majority of those I encountered simply wanting to feed off the feelgood factor that was in operation, men and women of all ages more than willing to share a beer and conversation, proud as they were that the biggest club game in European football had landed upon their expansive doormat.

Just off Taksim Square, those green buses continually rolled up, where they would be boarded by the thousands of Liverpool supporters who had made what would prove to be a pilgrimage to the club's first appearance in the final since the rebrand, repackaging, and expansion of the tournament by UEFA from the European Champion Clubs' Cup as it was, to the Champions League.

Next stop, the short hop to the Atatürk – we all thought, before experiencing a journey of endurance that at times felt as if it was without either direction or the hope of completion. A meander of a bus trip that seemed to take hours, sometimes with no more of a horizon that offered a rocky wilderness, without discernible landmarks and certainly no sign of a football stadium. It was the perfect metaphor for the path that Rafael Benítez's team had taken to reach this dizzying and unexpected situation. When would the journey end?

Travelling on what was effectively a greenhouse on wheels, and one with only minimal seating available, most on board had embraced this trial of endurance while standing up, steadily dehydrating, after an afternoon where the highly enjoyable Efes beer had been the liquid of choice for most. Knowing glances were shared with friends and strangers alike as we fought the shared pain of creaking bladders and no hope of emptying them anytime soon. The ebullient mood within the bus as we set off had been displaced by the kind of drained expressions you might see of the dwellers in an A&E waiting room during the witching hours of a Friday night into Saturday morning.

Rumbling onward up the steep incline of a particularly mountainous stretch of dual carriageway, unwittingly not too far from the Başakşehir Çam and Sakura City Hospital, travelling at not much more than walking pace, matters took an unexpected turn as the back window of the bus fell away, taking with it to the road outside one unfortunate passenger who had been perched on the back of the back row of seats, leaning against the defective glass pane.

Initial shock that reverberated around the bus was soon replaced by relief, then hilarity, when the ejected passenger reappeared at the now gaping hole at the back of the bus, from where he was pulled back up by his mates to be embraced and backslapped aplenty, the nonplussed driver having pulled up at the side of the road to peruse the damage to his vehicle.

Critical levels having been reached on bladder containment issues, with the bus now static the sight of two lads on the embankment relieving themselves was my own personal last straw, and handing my rucksack to Sue, one of the friends I was on this odyssey with, I alighted to answer the increasingly loud call of nature. It was the sweetest of moments, but one that was punctuated by shouts from the bus of Big Andy, another member of our group, alerting me that the driver had set off once again, leaving me with little other option than to wave them onwards with my free hand while I continued to water the arid and dusty embankment.

Consoled by the thought that at least two other passengers from the bus had also been marooned, it came as a bit of a surprise to see them both head towards a taxi that had also pulled up at the side of the road, unseen from my previous spot within the bus, to jump back into the vehicle they had just climbed out of.

As I stuck my head through the front passenger window to see if they had space for one more, while the four paying customers all shook their heads the taxi driver, who had seen this inglorious situation unfold, was very much up for the challenge of reuniting me with my travelling party. Heroically overruling his patrons, he insisted that I sit myself between the driver's and front passenger's seats, from where it was foot down and hot pursuit.

My mobile phone was ringing incessantly as Big Andy attempted to get word through to me that you could see the stadium in the distance from the top of the next peak, but the signal was so fragile that every time I pressed to accept his call the connection immediately cut out. On the bus, the urgent sense of panic among my friends had at least been downgraded to mild concern, primarily given that Sue was now in possession of my passport and return flight ticket, although I had been conscientious enough to secrete my match ticket safely on myself. Priorities are priorities, after all.

This communication breakdown was to continue as the taxi overtook the bus upon the approach to the stadium, eventually coming to a grinding halt in a build-up of other traffic. Out I bundled, my fellow unwilling passengers looking far from impressed, while the taxi driver was utterly delighted with his successful car chase. As I sat myself on a stone wall at the side of the road, the bus pulled up, and off stumbled Big Andy, with phone attached to ear, looking into the far distance from where they had travelled, still hoping to get through to me to reassure me that no more than half an hour or so of walking would likely get me there.

Big Andy was followed off the bus by Sue, Gary, Anthony, Martin, Stevie, Alison and her boys; all were mouth-open stunned to spot me sat serenely on the stone wall, perplexed that the person they had seen left behind a few miles up the road, just minutes earlier, was now sat before them asking what on earth had kept them, our heroic taxi driver with a prime sightline to see this bemusing interlude reach its happy conclusion.

Hugs dispensed, tales of derring-do recounted, introductions of friends to heroic taxi drivers done, it was at this very point that I knew Liverpool simply could not lose the game that was set to be played out in this state-of-the-art, if generally uninspiring, stadium that looked as if it had been built upon the surface of the moon.

Amid this, I was by no means alone in having to take an unorthodox route to the Atatürk, as all along the road towards it there were taxis aplenty that had crowbarred in extra passengers simply by throwing open their boots to act as makeshift seats, with the beers continuing to flow.

Outside the Atatürk, the party atmosphere continued. Famed Liverpool native and singer Pete Wylie was banging out the tunes on a temporary stage, turning his iconic song 'Story of the Blues' into 'Story of the Reds' for the occasion, and at the end of his set list the stage was swamped by revellers, prompting an overly dramatic safety officer to scream, 'Please get off the stage, or you will all die. It is falling down; I can see that it is falling down. You must get off now!'

Of course, my theory that we simply could not lose was to be stretched to the very limits by half-time, as Liverpool trailed 3-0 against a star-studded Milan, making for a chastening 45 minutes that had left home feeling an exceptionally long way away, and a handful of foolhardy individuals so bereft that they started their return journey with immediate effect. For the thousands upon thousands of Liverpool fans who stayed put at the Atatürk, however, a hymn of hope was boomed out at the interval, as 'You'll Never Walk Alone' was offered up almost as a sombre prayer rather than a defiant club anthem.

What came next was the Champions League's finest hour as Rafael Benítez sent out his beleaguered yet rearranged and reenergised team to pull off the impossible dream, completing one of the most improbable comebacks in football history, all due to the drive and determination of the Scouse duo of Steven Gerrard and Jamie Carragher, the vision of Xabi Alonso, and the tireless contributions of a collective in red that included a significant number of players who had no real future at Anfield beyond the summer.

In Istanbul, the miracle really did happen, and for those of us who were there to see it we will take the memories to our dying days, yet Liverpool winning the 2004/05 Champions League was so much more than one wild and dusky evening in Başakşehir: it was the entire journey to get there too, from a two-legged third qualifying round against Austrian opponents, the first leg of which was overshadowed by the impending departure of Michael Owen to Real Madrid, followed by the second leg which was a loss on home soil, before a group stage where home wins on the opening and closing nights bookended four games where not one Liverpool player managed to find the back of the net.

Oh, and beyond all that chaos, there was a knockout stage that saw Bayer Leverkusen, Juventus, and Chelsea dealt with, all amid a season when the team from Anfield could barely put two steps in front of one another domestically without tripping over their own laces, making for a tumultuous but also torturous season at times, under a new manager who had swept into the club after three spectacular years at the helm of Valencia.

So yes, the green bus that ferried us from Beyoğlu to Başakşehir was indeed the only fitting manner in which to travel from Taksim Square to the Atatürk for a Champions League Final that sat at the end of a campaign in which the back window of the Liverpool team coach had figuratively fallen out at one point when juddering up a steep incline, Gerrard having fallen out of the vehicle for a while, and Alonso having been marooned at the roadside, before launching a miraculous return.

Over two decades on, the story of Liverpool's 2004/05 Champions League success, quite gloriously, still doesn't make sense, and long may it not.

Chapter One
Ged the Red

CHRISTMAS 2003 was a miserable one for Liverpool. Sat ninth in the Premier League, 15 points adrift of leaders Manchester United, they were just eight points clear of the relegation zone, while the defence of their League Cup had already been ended when beaten at home by Bolton Wanderers in early December.

Sixteen league games into the 2003/04 season, Gérard Houllier's side had contrived to lose six of them, four of these defeats coming at Anfield; not only were Liverpool sat behind Alex Ferguson's reigning champions, along with Arsène Wenger's invincible-to-be Arsenal, Claudio Ranieri's suddenly rouble-rich Chelsea, and Bobby Robson's much-admired Newcastle United, but also the lesser lights of Chris Coleman's Fulham, Gordon Strachan's Southampton, Alan Curbishley's Charlton Athletic, and Steve Bruce's Birmingham City.

This was a Liverpool team that was the very epitome of inconsistency, one which would stumble two steps forward, stagger one back, and lurch one to the side all season long, in what was an almost shamefully successful mission to obtain Champions League qualification, finishing four points ahead of the now equally dysfunctional Newcastle and an overreaching Aston Villa, yet a mammoth 30 points adrift of eventual champions Arsenal.

The Gunners' unbeaten league campaign had been a truly remarkable achievement, yet it was set against a backdrop of a poor collective Premier League vintage in which Liverpool, although rolling over the finish line in fourth, ended up three points closer to relegation than they did to the champions, this during a season in which they wound up only seven points better off than Bolton and Charlton, and collected four points fewer than they had 12 months earlier when finishing one position lower, in fifth. Liverpool's 2003/04 points haul was their third lowest since three points for a win had been introduced.

Across the span of the season, while there was no shame in seeing Arsenal complete a league double over Houllier's team, it was utterly numbing that both Charlton and Southampton would claim the same notoriety too, within a campaign where Liverpool's best winning run stalled at three successive victories and their longest unbeaten run stretched to just six games.

In the FA Cup, Liverpool were unseated in a fifth-round replay at Portsmouth on a day when Michael Owen missed a penalty with the scoreline still goalless, while in the UEFA Cup they were eliminated in the last 16 by a Didier Drogba-inspired Marseille.

Worryingly, Liverpool's response to being knocked out of the UEFA Cup was to win just one of their next five Premier League fixtures, the nadir being a 1-0 defeat at home against Charlton on Easter Monday, a loss that left Houllier and his players only five points ahead of tenth-placed Fulham, with the west London side due next up at Anfield five days later for a game that ground its way to a lacklustre goalless draw, with this time Steven Gerrard guilty of missing from the spot.

Somehow Liverpool then clicked back into gear, picking up wins at Old Trafford and St Andrew's, sandwiching these awayday victories by taking three points at home to Middlesbrough. Combined with results elsewhere, bewilderingly it meant that Liverpool had clinched Champions League qualification with one game to spare.

On the final day it was back to general mediocrity, the curtain finally falling on a forgettable season with a 1-1 draw against Newcastle at Anfield, one in which Liverpool had trailed at half-time, and so uninspired where a significant number of those in attendance that they opted not to hang around for the customary end-of-season lap of honour.

For three players in red that afternoon, it was to prove to be the last time that they would play a competitive game for the club, not all of them moving on entirely by choice, as while we had almost knowingly witnessed Owen's departure unfold in slow motion for the previous 12 months or so, neither Danny Murphy nor Emile Heskey would have longed for their respective summer transfers to Charlton and Birmingham, at a time when both players were approaching what should have been their peak years, certainly in terms of age.

There would also be other reluctant departures that summer in the shape of the manager, his assistant, and an assortment of further coaching staff, with the curtain falling on Houllier's reign on 24 May 2004 after what had been nine days of deliberations and expectancy about a parting of the ways, ever since the Newcastle game had brought the season to an end.

As Liverpool supporters attempted to sooth their woes over the Christmas of 2003, it seemed incredulous to think that not much more than a year earlier the club had been sat at the top of the Premier League, unbeaten and momentarily seven points clear, with a third of the 2002/03 season almost navigated.

On 2 November 2002, Liverpool defeated West Ham United at Anfield, a 2-0 victory garnered by a goal in each half by Owen for what was a seventh successive league win, this on an afternoon when Gerrard's contribution was restricted to the final 21 minutes after he was introduced from the bench in place of the withdrawn Vladimír Šmicer.

Not all was as it might have seemed, however. Less than 72 hours earlier, a more telling representation of the underlying condition of Houllier's Liverpool had been laid bare at Anfield in the Champions League when facing Rafael Benítez's Valencia, just over five weeks beyond having been soundly dismantled by the same opponents at the Estadio de Mestalla.

In Spain, Liverpool had slipped to a 2-0 defeat on an evening when Houllier's side were restricted to just two significant opportunities, one in the first half when

Heskey was played in by Jamie Carragher – rounding Santiago Cañizares only to clip the far post from an acute angle – and a second-half chance that fell to Bruno Cheyrou in the penalty area after it was deflected into his path via a Dietmar Hamann free kick, only for Cañizares to be the equal of it.

On a night when Liverpool spent much of their time on the back foot, and defensive vulnerabilities were in sharp focus, Houllier's plans for the game were disrupted by Stéphane Henchoz's continued unavailability due to a calf strain he had sustained a week earlier, meaning that Salif Diao was deployed in central defence alongside Sami Hyypiä, only for the Senegalese World Cup star to be withdrawn at the interval, so tortured had he been by the effervescence of Pablo Aimar and bludgeoning presence of John Carew across the first 45 minutes.

While Houllier was backed into a corner in defensive terms, in the final third it was entirely optional when the decision was made to leave Owen and Milan Baroš sat among the substitutes rather than sending either of them out to start the game, with Heskey instead paired alongside the polarising figure of El Hadji Diouf. Just like his Senegalese compatriot Diao, Diouf did not reappear for the second half after Liverpool had been twice undone by the ruthless attacking incision of Aimar and the wonderful Rubén Baraja.

Composed, combative, fluid, totally at ease in possession of the ball and quick in all they did, Valencia were everything that Liverpool were not at the Mestalla, and by the time that the belatedly introduced Owen was lamenting being denied a blatant penalty in stoppage time, the gig had long been up as hopes of a late comeback were sunk as soon as Hamann was flashed a second yellow card and subsequent red with just over ten minutes remaining, the German international having allowed his frustrations get the better of him.

Although it was nothing more than the opportunity of a lost consolation goal, even after Owen's penalty claims had been waved away by the myopic referee Herbert Fandel, Valencia were soon off down the other end of the pitch, where Carew should have made it 3-0 but was denied by the reactions of Jerzy Dudek.

In his post-match comments, Houllier tried to reconcile the gulf in class between the two teams, left as he was to surmise that this hadn't been the real Liverpool and that his players were in the dressing room busy blaming themselves. Benítez, meanwhile, was decorum personified, stating that his opponents were a great team, just one that Valencia had successfully stopped from showcasing their strengths.

The evening had an unsavoury edge to it in the stands of the Mestalla, to go along with the chastening night that Liverpool had experienced on the pitch: Heskey, Diao, Diouf, and Djimi Traoré were the target of racist chants from Valencia supporters, chants which numbingly rolled around the famous old stadium with an ugly regularity, events combined that left a bitter taste in the mouth of the visitors, one which would still be evident when the two teams went up against each other once again at Anfield just over five weeks later.

To accentuate Houllier's theory that the real Liverpool hadn't presented itself at the Mestalla, across the eight games that his team played between the two fixtures against Valencia they won seven and drew one, five of these victories coming in the Premier League, inclusive of wins against Chelsea, Leeds United, and Tottenham Hotspur.

Ultimately damaging in the Champions League beyond the loss in Valencia, Liverpool had dropped further points during a 1-1 stalemate at Anfield against Christian Gross's Basel, on a frustrating night when Dudek was beaten with the first effort mustered on target by the reigning Swiss champions, Julio Rossi scoring resoundingly against the run of play shortly before the interval. This after Liverpool had largely laid siege to the Basel penalty area throughout the first half, Baroš having belatedly made the breakthrough in the 34th minute.

Three times Liverpool hit the frame of Pascal Zuberbühler's goal, also finding the Basel goalkeeper to be in the most outrageously inspired form. Near misses, goal-line clearances, and a clear penalty denied them when a Murphy free kick was handled by Christian Giménez, having been outclassed by Valencia the draw against Basel was a case of a misfortune most ludicrous, with a hint of profligacy thrown in for good measure.

Dominant back-to-back wins against Spartak Moscow in October put Liverpool's Champions League fate back in their own hands, with Valencia to come to Anfield, and a trip to Basel to follow, giving Houllier's team two chances to secure qualification for the second group stage.

When facing Valencia, it was a highly motivated Liverpool that spent 90 minutes banging their collective head against the brick wall that was Benítez's magnificently organised defence in a game that was settled by Francisco Rufete's deflected effort, which flicked off Hyypiä in the 34th minute, the ball deviating away from a trajectory that should have been easy enough for Dudek to deal with only for the Pole to be left stranded instead as it flew into his bottom-left corner.

This was a goal that undeniably stemmed from an excellent passing movement in which Liverpool were left chasing shadows, yet it was sealed with a finish that relied heavily upon good fortune. It would have been entirely in keeping with the game as a whole had Rufete's shot ambled past Hyypiä and rolled into the loving embrace of Dudek, a moment that was to be just another element of a shadow boxing goalless draw in the making.

On a fluctuating evening, at times Valencia were again the masters of possession while at other moments they were caught within a maelstrom in which a Liverpool equaliser seemed increasingly likely, at least until the determined and focused Heskey was perplexingly withdrawn on the hour and replaced by Baroš.

With Gerrard operating on the right of midfield, all too often finding himself isolated, John Arne Riise struggling to advance from his position at left-back, and Murphy suffering an off night, Owen was handed a largely thankless task that was only to become ever more cumbersome after the departure of Heskey.

However, this time it wasn't a cast-iron case of Valencia clearly outclassing Liverpool, although there were intermittent periods when the visitors did leave their opponents second best in midfield, especially whenever Aimar dropped deep; instead it was a game of punch and counterpunch, both sides having spells where they looked the more likely to take control of proceedings only for the flow of traffic to switch once again.

This was a game where Dudek and Cañizares were made to work, although each effort they were forced to deal with – apart from Rufete's deflected goal – could be classed as saves they should have been expected to make, chances that conversely the prospective goalscorers should have done better with. From a Liverpool perspective Gerrard and Owen were handed compelling sights of the whites of Cañizares's eyes only to plant their shots straight at the Spanish international, while a stooping Hamann header was cleared from danger, and Baroš was denied with a late opportunity.

In the opposite penalty area, Kily González clipped Dudek's crossbar with what appeared to be an attempted cross, and Baraja hastily ballooned a chance high into the Kop from six yards when closed down rapidly by Dudek, before the Liverpool goalkeeper also saved comfortably from Carew when the linesman's flag should have been raised for offside, a juxtaposition to an incident at the other end when Owen broke free on the left-hand side of the Valencia penalty area to bear down on Cañizares, only for the flag to be raised erroneously.

Baraja was to pass up on another opportunity during the second half, while Miguel Ángel Angulo stung the palms of Dudek from distance, yet in truth, the one goal aside, there wasn't a single true moment of peril at either end and Benítez must have been relieved as well as confused when he saw Heskey's number being lifted high by the fourth official, at a time when Liverpool had their most impressive spell of momentum rolling and the England striker had assumed the role as his team's chief facilitator.

A niggly game at times, animosity constantly bubbled beneath the surface, some of it lingering sentiment from Hamann's sending off at the Mestalla, and the still-incensed lynchpin of the Liverpool midfield was lucky to avoid a yellow card during the first half with Diao another to escape what would have been a warranted sanction, while for Valencia there were multiple occasions when Aimar should have been brandished a yellow, and David Albelda would have had no recourse to complain had he received a second caution and his marching orders for a lunge on Cheyrou, who had been thrown on in place of Carragher for the last ten minutes, an alteration by Houllier that saw Gerrard end the evening at right-back when his team was desperately in need of his inspiration in central areas instead.

Added to this negative chemistry, yet another ingredient to the simmering uneasy mood on the pitch between the two teams had been supplied by Carew during the build-up to the game when he successfully cast himself the villain of the Anfield piece with his pre-match comments that Liverpool would struggle to put themselves among the leaders of La Liga if they were playing their league football in Spain, and that Houllier's side were nothing more than a one-man team. It was with an admirable flourish of shithousery that Carew added by promising to score at Anfield, even ruffling Owen's hair when they passed one another during the handshakes prior to kick-off. He might not have got his goal, but Carew enjoyed the last laugh by being on the winning side.

As Houllier and his players limped away from this second loss to Valencia and on into the beginning of November, they at least had the solace that Benítez's team was still the only one to have inflicted defeat upon them so far during those opening months of the 2002/03 season and their immediate reaction was to win their next two domestic games, picking up three more Premier League points with a 2-0 victory against West Ham and then beating Southampton 3-1 to reach the fourth round of the League Cup, with both successes coming at Anfield.

But then came the defining on-pitch pivot of Houllier's aspirations, as within three days leading toward mid-November Liverpool's unbeaten start to their Premier League campaign came to an end in uninspiring circumstances at the Riverside Stadium against Middlesbrough, and a tumultuous 3-3 draw at St. Jakob Park with Basel marked their exit from the Champions League. It was to be a twin blow that would start the clock ticking on the endgame stretch of Houllier's Anfield reign.

At Middlesbrough, against a team who were enjoying their own fine start to the season on home soil but labouring on their travels, Houllier opted for an overly cautious approach, a lack of boldness that only resulted in Liverpool becoming progressively more negative as the afternoon wore on, until a glaring and costly error from Dudek gifted the only goal of the game to Gareth Southgate.

Three days later in Switzerland, Liverpool calamitously found themselves 3-0 down within 29 minutes against Basel, Houllier uncharacteristically throwing caution to the wind this time as he again got the balance of his approach to the game wrong, an expansive line-up finding itself cut to shreds by Gross's almost over-prepared players.

Gross had spirited his squad away to the Black Forest for an intensive training camp ahead of the clash with Liverpool, where alongside their regular doses of stamina and ball work they were subjected to a gruelling menu of watching endless videos of Houllier's team, followed by lectures and tests to see just what they had absorbed from these classroom sessions.

Less than half an hour in, the payoff for Basel's meticulous groundwork was writ large, as a punch-drunk Liverpool were left reeling from the goals scored by Rossi, Giménez, and Timothée Atouba, the initial breakthrough coming in only the second minute, as Gross's team grasped the nettle in spectacular fashion, showing no signs whatsoever of tentatively playing for the draw that would be good enough for them to progress.

Three goals adrift at the interval, Houllier stunningly withdrew an admittedly out-of-sorts Gerrard, replacing him with Diao, and while it was a massively contentious switch, collectively Liverpool did eventually click into gear, dragging themselves level at 3-3 thanks to goals from Murphy, Šmicer, and Owen, only to fall narrowly short of a place in the second group stage that on paper had looked theirs for the taking when the draw was made.

This was 90 minutes of chaos, wild swings that exposed the fragilities that lay beneath the surface of Liverpool's defence, yet an hour and a half that also demonstrated their potential powers of recovery when finding themselves in a desperate situation and the handbrake of caution was finally removed.

Clawing their way back to just a goal behind Basel when Murphy and Šmicer struck within three minutes of one another from the hour mark, with 27 minutes left in which to complete their attempted comeback Liverpool slipped back into a misfiring mode, Owen's equaliser not coming until the 85th minute and even then only after converting the rebound of a penalty he had seen saved by the again inspirational goalkeeping of Zuberbühler.

Fine lines and narrow margins: Liverpool had come close to pulling off a great escape act but the position they had found themselves in, both in terms of that evening in Basel and the wider landscape of Group B, was that their fate had been entirely of their own making, and in failing to beat either Basel or Valencia home or away, it was also totally deserved.

In many respects, the routes taken at the two most pronounced forks in the road for Liverpool in Basel were dictated by the two respective goalkeepers, as big shot-stopping first-half moments came when Houllier's team trailed 1-0, where an outstretched Zuberbühler managed to palm away a powerful effort from Heskey on to his crossbar from where it bounced away to safety, followed down the other end at 2-0 when Dudek's one-handed save from a rasping free kick by Hakan Yakin was parried not away and to his right but instead diagonally toward the angle of his six-yard box, where the perfectly positioned Atouba was able to take advantage, guiding the ball past the despairing Pole for 3-0.

On the back of his costly error at Middlesbrough, Dudek was suddenly under greater scrutiny and the worst was yet to come for him, while collectively the wheels didn't just begin to wobble for Liverpool, they spectacularly flew off as that first Premier League reversal of the season at the Riverside was to stunningly be the opening gambit in a run of 11 league games without a win, with Dudek suffering his personal nadir at the start of December when inexplicably and embarrassingly allowing the ball to run through him, handing a regularly profligate Diego Forlán his moment of iconography for Manchester United, events that resulted in Houllier's goalkeeper losing his place to Chris Kirkland.

From being sat comfortably atop the Premier League in November, two months later, when Liverpool walked out at St Mary's to finally put their winless league run to an end against Southampton, they had dropped down to seventh, one place behind Everton.

A soaring take-off followed by a steep nosedive; Liverpool's league form eventually levelled out enough for them to put themselves in the running for Champions League qualification as the 2002/03 season drew toward its climax. The victory over Southampton began a run of 13 league games from which Houllier's side gleaned nine wins, a span of time in which they also triumphed in the 2003 League Cup Final, defeating Manchester United on a day of redemption for Dudek at the Millennium Stadium in Cardiff.

This represented some much-needed better form, but it was still a spell in which mishaps bubbled to the surface as during this time Liverpool were tipped out of the FA Cup in a fourth-round replay at Anfield by a mid-table First Division side Crystal Palace, opponents who had not won a league game since the start of the new year. They also dropped into the UEFA Cup but those hopes were also ended on home soil, this time by Martin O'Neill's Celtic.

With two league games remaining, a Champions League place was Liverpool's to claim, but in their penultimate fixture Houllier was to be haunted by a man who he passed on the option to sign on a permanent deal a year earlier, after a promising five-month loan from Paris Saint-Germain.

Nicolas Anelka's two late goals for Manchester City at the Kop end were a hammer blow, not only turning a winning position for Liverpool into a defeat in their last home game of the season but also delivering Houllier the perfect riposte to the snub the former Arsenal and Real Madrid striker had suffered when a proposed full-time transfer to Anfield fell through.

A week later, another loss sustained, another lead squandered: Liverpool were beaten at Stamford Bridge by Chelsea, the west Londoners instead clinching Champions League qualification. They were soon to be acquired by Roman Abramovich, with the whole vista of English football upon the eve of immense landscaping.

A turbulent season, 2002/03 had started with such hope and potential for Liverpool only for it to self-destruct as winter began to make itself felt; an excellent foundation was too easily torn asunder and so much of this violent regression felt unnecessary. Houllier's summer 2002 transfer activities were swiftly to become a millstone around his neck that was repeatedly brought into pre-match pub discussions and on post-match radio phone-in shows, while journalists grew increasingly scathing with Glenn Moore, in his post-season review in *The Independent*, lambasting the Anfield efforts of what he declared to be a team that had cost £80m to assemble, and were reputedly the highest-paid collective in the Premier League.

At Stamford Bridge, the 90 minutes that unfolded against Chelsea projected an unerring synopsis of Liverpool's Premier League campaign as a whole, with the pleasing start of scoring the opening goal being enveloped by a lamentable middle section and a frustrating finale that was even presented with the top hat of a red card being brandished at Gerrard.

Defeat to Chelsea and the subsequent loss of Champions League football for 2003/04 was basically a form of relegation from UEFA's top table, a costly failure for Liverpool of an estimated financial hit of a projected £15-20m, at a time when chairman David Moores and his chief executive Rick Parry were openly courting avenues of fresh investment.

Stamford Bridge was merely the culmination of a series of careless events, as while there had been two defined periods of the season where Liverpool had found rich seams of prosperity, there was simply no avoiding the fact that that 11-game run without a league win and their worst home record for almost half a century were the overarching reasons for them falling short of the minimum requirement for continued expansion, in obtaining Champions League qualification.

It had all been so different 12 months earlier when Liverpool ended 2001/02 by reaching the 80-point barrier, finishing ahead of Manchester United for the first time in the league for 11 years, albeit still seven points adrift of champions Arsenal, while also impressing during a run to the quarter-finals of the Champions League.

Still, despite the relative merits of Liverpool's progress during 2001/02, there were caveats at play, with critical analysis often deeming Houllier's style of play to be too defensive-minded or too counterattacking, assessments that made their second-leg capitulation at the BayArena against Bayer Leverkusen in the Champions League quarter-final completely perplexing, on an evening when they conceded three times in the last 27 minutes, the withdrawal of Hamann on the hour certainly not helping the outcome.

A tale of what might have been; Houllier had admirably insisted that his team stood just ten games from greatness as the firing pistol was sounded on the 2001/02 run-in, only to see Arsenal put in a faultless Premier League sprint finish to claim the prize, part of an incredible unbeaten run from Wenger's team that stretched across their last 21 league games in which they dropped only six points from a possible 63, beginning with a victory at Anfield just before Christmas, whereas across the same span of fixtures Liverpool dropped 19 points.

More damagingly for Liverpool's hopes, however, was their nine-game Premier League run from early December to late January in which they picked up just one win, essentially a prototype for their 2002/03 stretch of 11 league games without a win, while it could also be argued that their second-half unravelling in Leverkusen was to be the perfect pointer for the first half Basel inflicted upon Houllier's defence that following season. In this respect, it was ironic that what was billed as Liverpool's strength, their defensive strength, was to be their weakness two seasons running in the Champions League.

Timing is everything in football, and for Liverpool in 2001/02 they too put in a magnificent run-in once they had returned to winning ways in the Premier League, claiming three points at Old Trafford, in what was the second act of a triumvirate of Danny Murphy-clinched victories at the home of Manchester United, a win that set in motion the accumulation of 41 of a possible last 45 points.

Fortune simply failed to smile upon the 2001/02 Liverpool when it came to the Premier League, the 80 points they gained having been the same number with which Alex Ferguson's side had been crowned champions 12 months earlier, and more than the tallies with which United had prevailed in 1996/97 and 1998/99, with Arsenal's 1997/98 total also weighing in in the upper 70s.

In a tantalising glimpse of what could have been, Liverpool's Premier League sliding door was complimented by the Champions League one with Lúcio's 84th-minute clincher for Leverkusen denying Houllier and his team a two-legged semi-final shot at a Manchester United team they had completed a league double over that campaign. Rather than being viewed as a double disappointment, the mood music spoke of looking toward going one step further the following season.

While 2001/02 was ultimately all about the narrow shortcomings of Liverpool, it was utterly ludicrous that they came so close to such big moments in the Premier League and Champions League at all given the events at Anfield on 13 October 2001.

David O'Leary's Leeds United were the visitors for a fixture to a rivalry that had been reawakened in recent seasons, with both teams enjoying something of a renaissance, bringing with it a competitive edge that hadn't consistently existed in games between the two clubs since the mid-1970s when the legendary Shankly-Revie duels would often dictate the destiny of the big prizes.

Leeds had been the opposition on the day that Houllier first led Liverpool on a solo basis, after the departure of Roy Evans had ended their short and bewildering co-management of the club, and across the span of the 1999/2000 and 2000/01 seasons Houllier and O'Leary had traded Champions League qualifying blows with one another, sharing some epic Premier League encounters, inclusive of that stunning Mark Viduka-inspired 4-3 defeat at Elland Road.

On this occasion, however, neither team were clicking into gear as the first half became littered with poorly directed passes and the regular sound of an unnecessarily overactive referee's whistle, the monotony of the footballing fayre punctuated only by Harry Kewell opening the scoring with the aid of a deflection.

It was in the Liverpool dressing room at the interval where matters took a dramatic turn as, having complained of chest pains, Houllier, rather than returning to the touchline for the second half, was instead rushed by ambulance to the Royal Liverpool Hospital at the insistence of the club doctor, Mark Waller, whose swift actions were crucial.

Upon assessment at the Royal Liverpool, the gravity of the situation soon became apparent and Houllier was transferred to Broadgreen Hospital's cardiothoracic unit, where he underwent an 11-hour operation to replace a section of his dissected aorta.

The news shocked Merseyside and beyond, bringing with it on one hand great concern for Houllier's health and wellbeing, with his very mortality brought into initial doubt, and on the other hand uncertainty for the Liverpool players and coaching staff.

Thankfully, the operation was deemed a success, and for the next five months Phil Thompson ably stood in as caretaker manager, with Houllier soon offering pointers during his convalescence. After much external conjecture over whether or not Houllier would be able to return to his role, he eventually slipped out of the Anfield tunnel and into the welcoming embrace of Fabio Capello in mid-March when Roma arrived for their decisive Champions League second group stage game, when a place in the quarter-finals was the prize being fought over.

During Houllier's absence he was still clearly active in pulling strings, with the £12m sale of Robbie Fowler to Leeds at the end of November and three weeks later that loan arrival of Anelka, alongside the signing of Baroš from Banik Ostrava, plus the surprise late-January purchase of Abel Xavier from Everton.

Any thoughts that Houllier's health scare would slow him down were soon dispelled, and if anything, when he did return to his post on a full-time basis it seemed as if it was with even greater intensity than before, which was perhaps the key to his eventual downfall at the end of the 2003/04 season.

Going into 2001/02, Houllier's Liverpool were in excellent condition, a club rejuvenated from the rut they had found themselves within as they headed into the summer of 1999. The cup treble of League Cup, FA Cup, and UEFA Cup in 2000/01 had exceeded all hopes and expectations, complimented as they were by pipping Leeds to Champions League qualification on the final day away to Charlton Athletic.

Suddenly, this was a Liverpool that had reacquainted themselves with the thrill of the chase for honours, and the 2000/01 run-in really felt like Houllier had turned back the clock to the glory days of Shankly, Paisley, Fagan, and Dalglish, days that were beginning to drift into an increasingly sepia-tinged past, mocked as we were by rival supporters for an increasing fixation on our history given that our contemporary efforts had been so lacking.

When we made the trip to Cardiff for the 2001 League Cup Final, it was in ungainly fashion that Liverpool took the trophy via a penalty shoot-out against First Division Birmingham City. An awkward success, but one that was embraced enthusiastically by those decked out in red, this was only Liverpool's third major honour since the resignation of Kenny Dalglish a decade earlier.

The aesthetics of the win over Birmingham aside, beggars couldn't be choosers, and after six years without a major trophy, the taste of success was infectious as Houllier and his players swept to the FA Cup and UEFA Cup finals too, returning to Cardiff to ram-raid Arsenal in the final few minutes of the former and being pushed all the way by Deportivo Alavés in the latter to a late Golden Goal, extra-time winner in Dortmund.

With Charity Shield and UEFA Super Cup successes obtained against Manchester United and Bayern Munich respectively, added in August 2001 to the cup treble that had been completed in May, it was with a sense of ruthlessness that Houllier soon replaced his goalkeeper Sander Westerveld with not one, but two alternatives, in Dudek and Kirkland, while Robbie Fowler made that departure to Leeds.

Driven, newly successful, and merciless, Houllier had worked a swift miracle in turning Liverpool's fortunes around from the sorry state they had appeared to be in at the end of the 1998/99 season as they limped to a seventh-placed finish in the Premier League and headlong into a summer in which Steve McManaman left on a Bosman-facilitated free transfer to Real Madrid.

In the summer of 1999, McManaman was followed through the Anfield exit door by other significant squad members: David James, Rob Jones, Paul Ince, Øyvind Leonhardsen, and before long Karl-Heinz Riedle too, as well as the oft-maligned Bjørn Tore Kvarme, with Steve Harkness and Jason McAteer having already been moved on. In a sweeping of the decks, among others, Houllier recruited Westerveld, Hyypiä, Henchoz, Hamann, Šmicer, Titi Camara, Erik Meijer, and into the new year, Heskey too.

Even in the lead-up to the cup treble campaign itself, and also during it, Houllier was bold in his rebuilding plans, with Brad Friedel, Stig Inge Bjørnebye, Steve Staunton, Phil Babb, Dominic Matteo, and David Thompson all either cashed in on, or cut loose on a free transfer, while the manager proved he wasn't fazed at all by the concept of quickly letting go of players he himself had signed, when Camara and Meijer were sold, as was one of Houllier's very early signings, Rigobert Song.

To offset this latest swathe of departures, in came Markus Babbel, Christian Ziege, Gary McAllister, Bernard Diomède, Igor Bišćan, Jari Litmanen, and explosively, Nick Barmby, sourced from just across Stanley Park, snatched from the clutches of Everton after he had been part of Kevin Keegan's England squad at the 2000 European Championship finals.

That Houllier managed to deliver the trophies he did while within the eye of such an intensive period of squad regeneration represented a project at Anfield that was way ahead of its anticipated plotline, which while absolutely glorious for Liverpool and their jubilant supporters, simply meant that expectations escalated to ultimately unattainable levels.

When Houllier was unable to deliver the dream of Premier League or Champions League glory during 2002/03 and 2003/04, even the fact he almost lost his life while on duty was not enough for either the club or a sizeable section of the support to maintain their once unshakable faith in him.

Clear backward steps were made and Houllier's decision making started to be questioned more and more, bringing with it a critical scrutiny that came into ever-sharpening focus as results took a turn for the inconsistent, a situation that eventually led to his departure in May 2004, thus paving the way for the arrival of Rafael Benítez.

Houllier had shown everyone associated with Liverpool a glimpse of the promised land, with the cup treble of 2000/01, and then positioning the club ten games from greatness the following season. He had been bold with that infamous statement during the run-in of 2001/02, and although the quote was used to mock Houllier over the years to come, he wasn't actually wrong in voicing his sentiment toward the possibilities in front of his team, a sentence he actually uttered with the word 'hopefully' as its precursor.

For Liverpool's supporters, and surely for the players too, after two years largely stuck in reverse gear between the summers of 2002 and 2004 the wounds of the regression of the team from the high levels of belief and potential it was riding two years before the exit of Houllier and the arrival of Benítez were undeniably festering. There was deep sadness over the way things had drifted under Houllier across his last two seasons at Anfield, but the feeling that it was time for change was overpowering.

In essence, the Houllier era was an intricate five-part saga, from his short partnership with Roy Evans, onward to the regeneration and modernisation of the club with Phil Thompson as an assistant who was able to keep everything grounded in the tradition that was the fabled Liverpool Way, followed by the cup treble season, before his health issues of October 2001 marked a sweet and sour divergence that ran until the November of 2002, from when regression then stunningly began to take root, the germination of which came at a time when Liverpool were sat atop the Premier League.

After the highs of May 2001, anything seemed possible for Houllier and Liverpool, and while it was painful that Arsenal remained one step ahead in the 2001/02 Premier League title race, and as disappointing as the Champions League quarter-final second leg unravelling in Leverkusen was, these near misses had an air of a dress rehearsal and most of us were philosophical about them, because we felt like such successes were merely being delayed for now, a theory that was only given more legitimacy by a fine start to the 2002/03 Premier League campaign.

From November 2002 onward, however, when the wheels began to come off, it was a case of the promised land drifting out of reach once again, and after we had seemed within touching distance of it those near misses of 2001/02 began to sting much more than they initially had at the point of impact, as did Houllier's transfer dealings of the summer of 2002, particularly the passing on permanently signing Anelka and the added release of Litmanen while the cohort of new arrivals failed to impress.

A case of what gloriously was, in terms of 2000/01, offset by the agony of an unrequited tilt at even bigger prizes in the three seasons to follow, Houllier had taken Liverpool to the very doors of potential Premier League and Champions League glories only to misplace the keys to open them up once we'd arrived.

In the final reckoning, going into the winter of 2002/03, Houllier's moment to produce such successes had unwittingly gone and all that was left until his May

2004 departure was a thankless task to chase Liverpool's no longer wagging tail. The club was in need of fresh impetus and a new direction in which to travel.

Chapter Two

All Hail the Rafatollah

IN THE summer of 1998, as Liverpool and Gérard Houllier were gravitating toward one another, Rafael Benítez was basking in the glow of his greatest coaching achievement so far, fresh off the back of having led Extremadura to promotion from the Segunda División and returning them to the Primera División (La Liga) for only their second season of top-flight football.

Benítez had taken over at Extremadura in the summer of 1997, his appointment as head coach coming within the wake of the club's relegation to the Segunda having been one of the unfortunate victims of the reduction of La Liga's upper level from 22 to 20 teams for the 1997/98 season to come, a situation which eventually meant that five teams were relegated.

Arguably, it had taken a quirk of footballing bureaucracy for the Extremadura job to land in Benítez's lap, yet it was also a rebate of sorts, recompense for the events of two years earlier when his best-laid plans for his first coaching venture away from the rarified confines of the Santiago Bernabéu were undone, at least in part, due to his projected mission being radically altered just a month before the big kick-off. When unveiled as Valladolid's new head coach in the summer of 1995, the envisioned task at hand for Benítez was a bid to restore the club's Primera División status, which it had lost at the end of the 1994/95 season when trailing over the finish line in 19th position, ahead only of a highly dysfunctional Logroñés, who had managed to win just two of their 38 league games, scoring a pitiful 15 goals.

Chaos was to come, however, as while Benítez diligently built himself a team fit for the purposes of challenging for promotion from the Segunda, little more than a month from the start of 1995/96 season news broke from the Real Federación Española de Fútbol that Sevilla and Celta Vigo were to be summarily relegated from the Primera División due to a lack of financial transparency to the league and the delays on bond payments due from both clubs.

A can of worms was opened, and whether they were prepared for top-flight football or not, Valladolid and Albacete were abruptly reprieved from the relegations they were consigned to just six weeks earlier, while in riposte to the sanctions handed to them Sevilla and Celta Vigo were able to successfully cite the minutiae of Spanish law to obtain themselves an extra 15 days in which to get their finances in order, which both conscientiously did.

Backed into a corner, the Real Federación Española de Fútbol elected to allow all the clubs involved in the promotion and relegation debacle to have a place in the Primera División for the forthcoming 1995/96 season, thus enlarging the top flight to 22 teams for the next two seasons before reducing it once again to 20 in the summer of 1997.

Joy for the supporters and directors of Valladolid, but while Benítez was now handed the unexpected opportunity to test himself against the great and the good of Spanish football it was like going into a monsoon armed only with a cocktail umbrella; after overseeing 23 mostly punishing league games, Benítez was relieved of his duties toward the end of January, after a 5-2 defeat at home to Valencia.

Having won only twice across those 23 league games, Valladolid were bottom of the Primera División and nine points adrift of safety when Benítez departed, with the club bringing Vicente Cantatore back to the Estadio José Zorrilla for a third spell as head coach, from where he stunningly pulled off one of the greatest of escapes from what was a seemingly inevitable relegation.

On one hand, Benítez's failure at Valladolid had been entirely understandable given that when facing life in the Segunda, the club had offloaded players of the calibre of the double European Cup-winning sweeper Miodrag Belodedici, the defensive midfielder Javi Gracia, the rising talent of Iñaki Hurtado, the wondrous but ageing former Polish international Jan Urban, and his strike partner, the nomadic yet talented Brazilian, Nílson Esidio, all of whom were part of an exodus of 23 players. Yet, on the other hand, beyond the sacking of Benítez, Valladolid would go on to lose only four of their last 19 in the league, winning nine times, with the experience and know-how of Cantatore leading them to 16th position and salvation, ending up just one point behind Sevilla in 12th, in a blanket finish that included an 8-3 victory away to Real Oviedo on the penultimate weekend.

While the imbalance in Valladolid's results under Benítez compared to those of Cantatore across the 1995/96 season tell a damning story, Benítez's summer 1995 restructuring of the squad he inherited couldn't be faulted under the turbulent circumstances, with the recruitment on loan from Valencia of the future Real Madrid and Spanish international central defender Iván Campo being a shrewd decision, as were moves for Castilla defender José Luis Santamaría and creative midfielder Fernando Sánchez.

Added to these signings, Benítez deserved credit for recognising the goalscoring intuition of the Dinamo Zagreb striker Alen Peternac, but should have expected more from the talents possessed by another Croatian, midfielder Aljoša Asanović, although this disappointment was offset as Valladolid were blessed by the continuing emerging gifts of a 20-year-old by the name of Rubén Baraja.

Had Valladolid ended the 1994/95 season with the knowledge that they were going to be playing top-flight football in 1995/96, you would have to question if they'd have turned to Benítez as their choice to lead them given his complete lack of Primera División experience as either a player or a head coach.

In essence, there were two theories behind Benítez's struggles at Valladolid, as here was a man who had been unexpectedly dropped in at the deep end and undeniably floundered, with a squad that on paper seemed ill-equipped to prosper, yet his successor had performed wonders with the same set of players on grass. Despite having no shortage of technical knowledge, Benítez had been unable to inspire Valladolid's players in the manner Cantatore clearly could.

As part of this, Benítez's successor hadn't been any old random appointment, as in Cantatore Valladolid had turned to the man who had taken them to the 1989 Copa del Rey Final, where they were only narrowly beaten by the might of Real Madrid. Cantatore was a man who undoubtedly had the measure of his surroundings at Valladolid, in a way that Benítez, at this stage, simply didn't have the guile to match. Players are always going to be more confident when led by a coach who already has a track record for miracles when compared to one who is relatively fresh out of the blocks.

Prior to Valladolid, Benítez had very much been part of the furniture at Real Madrid, joining their youth system as a 13-year-old from where he displayed enough competency in the C team as both a sweeper and a midfielder to put himself on the brink of a breakthrough with Castilla, Real Madrid's Segunda-dwelling reserve side of great repute, until a knee injury derailed his progression.

While never likely to be good enough to play at the highest levels, Benítez was certainly robbed of the chance of stepping up to measure his abilities in the second tier of Spanish club football, and by the time of his return to fitness the window of opportunity for progression with Real Madrid had passed him by.

In the summer of 1981, within the weeks following Liverpool's victory over Real Madrid in the European Cup Final in Paris, Benítez accepted a loan move to the modest yet relatively ambitious Madrid club Parla, whom he helped to promotion from the Tercera División, Spain's fourth tier, gaining themselves entry to the Segunda División B for the first time in their so far brief history.

A club that had only been formed in 1973, with the step up to the third tier attained, in the Spanish World Cup summer of 1982 Benítez made his switch to Parla a permanent one and for the next three years he aided the club in largely holding their own as a mid-table entity, where he tested himself against teams who had punched at a higher weight, such as Albacete, Granada, Levante, and Rayo Vallecano.

Still attached to the apron strings of Real Madrid to an extent, in the summer of 1985 Benítez accepted a transfer to Linares, down in Andalucia, managed by Enrique Mateos, a former Spanish international striker and a double European Cup winner with *Los Blancos*, in 1957 and 1959, scoring the opening goal in the final of the latter.

At Linares, Benítez, by now in his mid-20s, combined playing with coaching duties, going on to become an assistant to Mateos, and when a recurrence of his earlier knee injury left him at a crossroads in 1986 he made the tough decision to retire as a player in order to focus fully on the coaching side, although rather than continuing this evolvement of his career with Linares, it was back to Real Madrid he went, where he got his foot on the bottom rung of the Bernabéu coaching ladder with the same Castilla youth teams he once played for.

For the next five years, Benítez led a variety of Castilla and Real Madrid youth age groups, working his way up to coach the under-19 side, combining his duties in this latest post by assisting Mariano García Remón with the Castilla first team before succeeding him as head coach in the summer of 1993, when Remón accepted an offer to take over at Sporting Gijón.

With Castilla barred from being promoted to the Primera División, Remón had essentially reached a notorious Real Madrid glass ceiling, where the only route to further progression for him was either to become the assistant to the Real head coach or to stretch his legs by taking on a position away from the Bernabéu, and two years later it was to be the turn of Benítez to take the plunge in opting to depart the Spanish capital having reached the very same plateau.

However, during those last two years at the Bernabéu, the learning curve for Benítez was a steep one, seconded as he was for the last two months of the 1993/94 season to assist Vicente del Bosque with Real Madrid after the sacking of Benito Floro, before returning to his role with Castilla again in the summer of 1994 when Jorge Valdano was appointed as Floro's successor, with Del Bosque resuming his position as number two.

At the helm of Castilla, Benítez led them to finishes of sixth and eighth in the Segunda in 1993/94 and 1994/95, admirable final positions, and along with these fine performances he was also to become the man who handed Raúl his first professional appearance, only to see the precocious teenager fast tracked into the Real Madrid first-team squad within days of an accomplished October 1994 debut in a defeat at Palamós.

It was a natural situation for other clubs to be eager to employ Benítez, and even his torrid time in charge of Valladolid did little to quell demand for his services, as in the summer of 1996 Osasuna offered him the seemingly perfect environment to blossom, at Estadio El Sadar.

In Pamplona, for Benítez the solid theory of a fantastic opportunity with a club that had been a top-flight staple throughout the 1980s and the first half of the 1990s clashed with the volatile practicalities of working under a demanding and unpredictable president, Juan Luis Irigaray having been the beneficiary of a power struggle that had ousted his predecessor, Javier Garro, himself not long having inherited the infinitely calmer waters created by the 23-year era of Fermín Ezcurra, a man who oversaw a golden period when the club travelled from the third tier to multiple European qualifications.

Osasuna had slipped out of the Primera División two years before the arrival of Benítez, with Garro sweeping to the presidency on the back of a campaign of positivity despite the club's 1993/94 relegation, only for 18 months of struggle to unseat him, Irigaray launching a compelling demand for significant change, Garro having previously been the long-term vice-president under Ezcurra.

Out of the frying pan and into the fire: under Irigaray, Osasuna would flirt with a return to the third tier, only recovering their composure after his own 1998 dethroning, and as part of this Benítez was to be the first of four head coaches that Irigaray would hire and fire across the span of the impressively combustible 1996/97 season.

Benítez would oversee just nine league games in charge of Osasuna, with the axe falling after a numbing loss away to lowly Écija in early November, on a day when the former Bolton Wanderers and future West Bromwich Albion striker Fabian de Freitas was flashed a red card shortly before half-time, thus stifling his team's hopes for a second half in which they conceded twice without mustering a reply.

In a chastening four months at the El Sadar, the biggest positive for Benítez was crossing professional paths with Pako Ayestarán for the first time, kicking off an enduring coaching partnership that would stretch on for the next 11 years, travelling a path that would lead them all the way to Anfield. It was also at Osasuna that Benítez absorbed his first experiences of coaching English players, having recruited the services of Robert Ullathorne and Jamie Pollock, and despite the brief nature of his time in Pamplona it was another valuable step along an increasingly varied learning curve.

Left with time to ponder the pitfalls he had encountered at Valladolid and Osasuna, Benítez was forced into football's shadows for the remainder of the 1996/97 season, not returning until the modest Extremadura offered him a way back in the summer of 1997 in succession to Josu Ortuondo, the man who had led the club into the top flight of the Spanish game for the first time in their history, although he had been unable to keep them there.

Extremadura's rise had been meteoric, going from fourth tier to top tier in just six years between 1990 and 1996, and Ortuondo's part in this was the second and third of that trio of promotions, so when relegation back to the Segunda befell them in 1996/97 it was understandable that offers of fresh challenges would not be in short supply, and it was to the also-relegated Rayo Vallecano that Ortuondo now headed, thus paving the way for Benítez's arrival at the Estadio Francisco de la Hera.

Fuelled by the goals of the Pichichi-winning Igor Gluščević, Extremadura fended off the threats posed by Las Palmas and Villarreal to finish runners-up to the determined, defensively strong, but pragmatic Alavés, with Benítez successfully proving that his coaching credentials had not been irrevocably damaged by his travails at Valladolid and Osasuna.

Yet, just as with Ortuondo two years earlier, the Primera División in 1998/99 for Extremadura under Benítez was to be a marginal bridge too far, with relegation back to the Segunda succumbed to via a two-legged play-off against Rayo Vallecano after finishing just one point behind Alavés, undone by a defined lack of goals, hamstrung after the sale of Gluščević to Sevilla, in a season during which Extremadura were the lowest scorers when netting only 27 times, their near-miss on survival coming down to a defence that conceded on fewer occasions than Real Madrid did.

Having now proved himself a coach of rich potential at Extremadura, Benítez recognised, just as Ortuondo had, that there was an unbreakable ceiling at the Estadio Francisco de la Hera, twice the club had climbed as high as it ever would, and that his future lay elsewhere. However, rather than jump straight into another post, Benítez opted to take himself upon a journey of enlightenment, travelling Europe on a watching brief of differing approaches and methods away from Spanish soil, imbibing the systems of any club of purpose that were willing to open up their doors to him.

One of these clubs was Manchester United, during which time Benítez struck up a friendship with Alex Ferguson's right-hand man, Steve McClaren, where conversational opportunities provided Benítez with further insights on both the complexities and occasional Anglo-Saxon basics of English football, all of which were to be invaluable for future reference, to go alongside his wider adherence to the influences of Arrigo Sacchi's Milan. A cosmopolitan melting pot was beginning to simmer away for a jobless man, who was less than five years away from claiming the Liverpool hot seat.

By the summer of 2000 Benítez was ready to resume his coaching career again, and he jumped at the opportunity offered to him by Tenerife, a club that had been a staple of the Primera División throughout the 1990s until their relegation to the Segunda at the end of the 1998/99 season. Just three years prior to Benítez landing his latest managerial position, Tenerife had narrowly missed out on reaching the 1996 UEFA Cup

Final, beaten narrowly by Schalke. Despite them now languishing in the second tier, this was a marked step up the managerial ladder for Benítez.

With a combination of technical excellence and aggression, pulling together a team that moved the ball fast and were swift to close down their opponents, armed with an ability to score within as few passes as possible, Benítez's Tenerife were blessed by attacking talent such as the future Valencia striker Mista, the Brazilian goalscorer Barata, and a Liverpool cult-hero-to-be in Luis García, forming the sharp end of a collective that were part of a big-hitting race for promotion as they edged out Atlético Madrid to finish third behind Sevilla and Real Betis.

This was a truly head-turning moment when it came to Benítez for other clubs, yet even so, it still came as something of a shock when Valencia swooped for his services, in the summer of 2001, as the successor to the departing Héctor Cúper, who after leading them to back-to-back Champions League finals in 2000 and 2001, had accepted an offer to take over at Internazionale.

Benítez was by no means Valencia's first choice as their new head coach; they had initially courted Javier Irureta, who had led Deportivo de La Coruña to the Primera División title during Benítez's gap year, Luis Aragonés, who had coached the club during the mid-1990s, and Mané, who had led Alavés to the 2001 UEFA Cup Final, before turning their attentions to the man in charge of Tenerife, impressed as the Valencia president, Pedro Cortes, was with the style of football that Benítez had initiated during their promotion campaign.

At face value, Benítez had seemed an underwhelming appointment by Valencia, and when added to the sale of Gaizka Mendieta to Lazio it felt as if they had been neutered as a threat, with the loss of a widely heralded, visionary coach, and one of the best players in the world hardly constituting a resounding strengthening of resolve for the new season ahead.

Yet Benítez opted for the role of the enabler, winning his new squad of players over by pointing out that as double Champions League finalists they already had all of the pedigree they needed, and while he had come to them from the Segunda he was utterly convinced that he could unlock the potential of a club that had not won the league for 30 years, and as runners-up in those two Champions League finals, had taken on the role of the bridesmaids of Europe.

From Tenerife, Benítez brought with him not only Ayestarán, but on the playing side he also plucked Mista, and the utility man Curro Torres, while the recruitments of Carlos Marchena and Francisco Rufete from Benfica and Málaga respectively were to be shrewd decisions. With the dressing room on Benítez's side, it wasn't long before the supporters were won over by a style of play that was more fluid and attractive than the variant that Cúper had spun.

Without Mendieta, Benítez was able to create a more balanced framework for Valencia, one which wasn't reliant upon overarching individuals, instead sharing the weight of the load across the entire team, with multiple options in all positions. It meant that the loss of any one given player would not mean the end of the world for the collective.

Reunited with Baraja, whom Benítez had coached at Valladolid as a teenager, and blessed by the presence of Pablo Aimar, the new man on the Valencia touchline could also call upon the likes of Miguel Ángel Angulo, John Carew, Kily González, Vicente Rodríguez, and Juan Sánchez, while security measures were dealt with by significant figures such as David Albelda, Roberto Ayala, Mauricio Pellegrino, and Amedeo Carboni, with the goalkeeping duties being blessed by the safe hands, determination, and no shortage of character of the excellent Santiago Cañizares.

Valencia won only seven of their opening 18 league fixtures of the 2001/02 season leading up to Christmas and the winter break, although they lost just twice, carving themselves something of a niche as draw specialists, but defeating Real Madrid on the opening day had banked Benítez a lot of immediate goodwill as had a 13-game unbeaten start to the league season. So, despite Valencia being sat seventh at Christmas, and momentum being sporadic, they were only three points behind the leaders, Irureta's Deportivo, with Real Madrid, Celta Vigo, Real Betis, Athletic Club, and Alavés sat between them, Barcelona labouring in eighth.

Eventually an inconsistent January, inclusive of a shock defeat at home to Valladolid, finally gave way to a 17-game run to the finish line in which Valencia lost only once, winning 13 times. Benítez's side clinched the Primera División title on the penultimate weekend after a

2-0 victory at Málaga, finally ending their 31-year league drought.

From a standing start of being an outlier of an appointment to the Valencia job, within a year Benítez had succeeded in a manner where a string of his high-achieving predecessors had failed to do at Estadio de Mestalla. Heriberto Herrera, Marcel Domingo, Miljan Miljanić, Guus Hiddink, Carlos Alberto Parreira, Luis Aragonés, Jorge Valdano, Claudio Ranieri, and Héctor Cúper could boast domestic titles or cup successes aplenty throughout the biggest leagues across Europe and South America, while in Parreira, Valencia had even been led by a World Cup-winning coach.

A moment of supreme glory for Valencia in 2001/02, the following season represented something of a loose hangover for the club – at least during the run-in – as they managed to win only four of their last 15 in the league to not only relinquish their crown as champions but also to slip outside of the Champions League berths, this from being within touching distance of the title race as February came to an end, while in the Champions League in 2002/03 Benítez had taken Valencia to the quarter-finals, where they bowed out on away goals against Internazionale.

A fade-out that raised fresh questions about Benítez, his response was a series of modest recruitments, with the arrivals of Mohamed Sissoko from Auxerre, Fabián Canobbio from Peñarol, Jorge López from Villarreal, and Ricardo Oliveira from Santos, along with the return of Xisco from a year on loan at Recreativo de Huelva.

During a summer in which Real Madrid spent big on David Beckham, and Barcelona captured Ronaldinho, Ricardo Quaresma, and Rafael Márquez, just as in the close-season of 2001 it once again left Valencia looking like the poor relations, all the more so given that González had been sold to Internazionale, and Carew had been packed off to Roma for a season-long loan.

However, with Barcelona adjusting to the Frank Rijkaard era, and Real Madrid thrown together with Carlos Queiroz after the ill-judged removal of Vicente del Bosque, the relative stability between Valencia and Benítez would once again bear fruit. While Real Madrid spectacularly lost six of their last seven league games, Barcelona were always playing catch-up after a disjointed first half of their campaign.

In 2003/04 for Valencia it was all about sound defending, midfield vision, and incisive attacking as Benítez put together a wonderfully balanced team, with Baraja, Vicente, and Mista forming a triumvirate that made for irresistible viewing. The Primera División title was reclaimed with two games to spare, and the UEFA Cup was added a week and half later when they swept Olympique de Marseille aside at the Ullevi in Gothenburg.

Benítez had made Valencia one of the most attractive, respected, and feared teams in Europe, and in turn, while his players had become the envy of the great and the good of the continent, he himself had become hot property too. Less than a week beyond the 2004 UEFA Cup Final, Liverpool were in the market for a new manager.

Chapter Three

Self Grazification

AS SOON as Gérard Houllier made his exit from Anfield the long-existing rumours and counter-rumours over his projected successor went into overdrive, and with none of the names floated by the sports journalists of the United Kingdom seemingly willing to distance themselves from the post it became a situation that even had enough allure to attract José Mourinho's attention, at least momentarily, away from the vital business of Porto's impending Champions League Final against Monaco in Gelsenkirchen.

When asked about the vacancy at Anfield during one of his last press conferences before the biggest game of his career, Mourinho had been glowing in his admiration of Liverpool although, be that in an act of genuine interest in the position or him simply fluttering his eyelashes in another direction other than Stamford Bridge in a bid to provoke Roman Abramovich into upping his proposed salary at Chelsea was wide open to debate.

Cast against the Mourinho question, a defiant Jaime Orti, the Valencia president, was quoted in a Jason Burt article in *The Independent*, in reference to his double

Primera División-winning head coach, as saying, 'He will coach Valencia next season. I don't think these rumours have any substance,' a statement of intent which meant that Rafael Benítez initially seemed to be a less likely option for Liverpool than any of the other realistic runners and riders, Mourinho included.

In the very same article, Michael Owen had words attributed to him, saying, 'The board are quite capable of picking the next manager,' when attempting to play down wider intimations that he might have had a say in Houllier's departure, with conjecture over the extent of the levels of player power at Anfield in his unseating having long been a source of chatter.

Within three days of Houllier's exit, whether they felt threatened by Liverpool or not, Chelsea had escalated their chase of Mourinho and were confident that they had a deal tied up in the wake of Porto's Champions League success, while local media in Valencia was stating that Benítez was set to accept the opportunity of succeeding Houllier at Anfield, although this was offset with mixed messages abounding as the man himself was on Spanish radio stating his desire to stay at the Mestalla, under condition that the changes he wanted were implemented.

As things stood at this footballing poker table, Benítez and Mourinho had the strongest of hands to play, and while Houllier had made his departure at Liverpool before the process of courting a replacement had seriously commenced, at Chelsea Claudio Ranieri had been left to await his inevitable sacking for the best part of a month, ever since he had presided over the club's Champions League semi-final exit at the hands of Monaco, Abramovich unwilling to dispense with the much-liked Italian until his successor was secured.

Every day brought with it a fresh twist, and Valencia were starting to get increasingly twitchy, with contract talks being mooted by Orti – his head coach now sat with only one year left on his existing deal – and thus the stand-off began to take root as Benítez's agent Manuel García Quilón became ever more vocal about his client's situation.

Amid this simmering Merseyside and Valencian kitchen sink drama, the *Daily Express* claimed that Kenny Dalglish was waiting in the wings should Benítez stay at the Mestalla, although Didier Deschamps was also a speculated alternative, while lingering links to Alan Curbishley simply refused to evaporate, but the Charlton Athletic manager was now becoming a more distant prospect.

A week on from the departure of Houllier, and on the day that Chelsea finally sacked Ranieri, Liverpool chief executive Rick Parry stated that the club would not be making an announcement about a new managerial appointment for a fortnight, while on a busy news day, Brazilian great Rivaldo was linked with a move to Bolton Wanderers, the start of a protracted month-long flirtation that eventually came to nothing, with the player being extensively hawked around by his agent after a souring of relations with Milan and a short return to his homeland with Cruzeiro.

Amid a frustrating summer for the 33-year-old fading superstar, another prospective move to Qatar was a possibility, while Celtic were said to be willing to offer him a trial. Incensed by the concept of having to audition for a contract at Celtic Park, Rivaldo would instead end up at Olympiacos, with whom he would be part of a pivotal night at Anfield in the 2004/05 Champions League group stages.

At the very start of June, Benítez reached his tipping point with Valencia, departing in tears during his final press conference for the club after saying that he saw it as a positive that Orti had made attempts to keep him, but that interference in his work was a driving factor behind his decision to leave. True to Parry's word, it would still be another fortnight before he was unveiled by Liverpool, although all bets on Benítez being the new manager were essentially settled.

Despite this apparently now unavoidable union between Liverpool and Benítez, and with Mourinho having officially been appointed at Stamford Bridge, within 24 hours of his parting of the ways with Valencia the lack of swift and decisive action by Liverpool during those first two weeks of June opened the door to ambiguity on several levels.

As the days meandered on, even Benítez seemed nonplussed by the lack of movement from Liverpool, and when he was quoted about the impasse in *The Independent* it was enough to throw doubt on the situation once more. 'Winning a league and UEFA Cup in the same year are sufficient motives for a lot of clubs to put their attention my way, or to look at the players. However, my agent, who has the professional obligation to listen to every team, has told me there is nothing concrete with any of those teams. There is interest from various clubs, but nothing more. When my agent has weighed up the offers, he'll give me his thoughts, and we will decide if one of them is convincing enough.'

Added to this, the continuing lack of clarity in the manager's office was complimented by boardroom uncertainty, with Thaksin Shinawatra being on the brink of pulling the plug on his hopes and dreams of buying a 30 per cent stake in the club, plans that revolved around him raising money via a national lottery. For Benítez, when finally appointed, there would be a degree of jumping out of the Valencia frying pan and into the Merseyside fire.

It wasn't until 16 June that Liverpool and Benítez consummated their marriage, the announcement coming over a week since Claudio Ranieri had been appointed his successor at Valencia, the new manager full of smiles and positivity at his Anfield unveiling – this being in sharp contrast to his emotions upon departing Valencia.

Handed a five-year contract and the levels of control that he could only pine forlornly for at the Mestalla, Benítez was thrown straight into the tug-of-war that was Steven Gerrard's situation, with the Liverpool captain seemingly amenable to talking to Peter Kenyon over a prospective move to Chelsea, the west London club reputedly willing to triple the player's salary.

When signing his new contract in November 2003, Gerrard had settled upon a gentleman's agreement with Parry in which he would be allowed to move on if Liverpool did not appear to be making significant on-field progress, and with Chelsea prepared to part with £31m to secure his services, Gerrard's days at Anfield appeared to be diminishing in number.

Benítez was in a fighting mood, however, insisting that retaining Gerrard and Michael Owen was an immediate priority and that he was wanting to talk to them as soon as possible, a prospect that was muddied by them being on duty in Portugal with England at the 2004 European Championship finals, where Gerrard was exposed to the influence of Chelsea players John Terry, Frank Lampard, Joe Cole, and Wayne Bridge.

Within the formative days of Benítez's reign, the potential loss of Gerrard seemed much more realistic than that of Owen, despite the latter only having one year remaining on his contract, while the tantalising prospect of the new manager launching transfer raids on his former employers was spiked by Benítez himself when categorically stating that he would not be making any moves on Valencia players, something that would be of a bitter disappointment to Liverpool supporters who had been measuring up for Rubén Baraja and Pablo Aimar.

Benítez's words on the matter of his former players were still not enough to slow the rumour mill down, however, as the veteran striker Juan Sánchez was speculated as a possible recruit before completing a switch back to his former club Celta Vigo instead, while his fellow attacker Mista would be a heavily touted possibility for much of the summer.

With little in the way of a holiday, Benítez was soon heading to Portugal to intercept the England squad and introduce himself to Gerrard, Owen, and Jamie Carragher, and to reach out to Dietmar Hamann, and Stéphane Henchoz who were also at the finals with Germany and Switzerland respectively, along with Vladimír Šmicer and Milan Baroš, who were both in the Czech Republic squad.

For a man inheriting a collection of players at Anfield that were broadly accepted as needing both fresh impetus and a fair bit of pruning, Benítez must have been partially bemused to find seven of Liverpool's underachieving squad from the 2003/04 season on duty in Portugal (eight when you throw Emile Heskey into the equation, who had by now completed his move to Birmingham City). Bizarrely, there were as many current Liverpool players at the tournament as those of the *Galácticos*-encrusted Real Madrid.

Before he had even been able to get his feet under his new desk, Benítez was subjected to the oddities of the shadow puppetry of football journalism in the Premier League as a fantasy revolving door was constructed to help fill column inches, aimed at fuelling rapidly decreasing print sales on Merseyside and beyond. With only one year remaining on his contract, Dietmar Hamann was swiftly linked with a £1.5m transfer back to Bayern Munich; the player would stay with the Anfield club for another two years.

Within 48 hours of Benítez's unveiling, Phil Thompson was a departee, the last member of the coaching staff with an existing Liverpool background, bringing to an end the fabled Boot Room link that had begun almost half a century earlier, while as a teaser of how busy Benítez's inbox was going to be at Melwood, the following day the Thai business magnate Paiboon Damrongchaitham was linked to stepping into the void to buy the 30 per cent stake in Liverpool that Shinawatra was no longer pursuing.

Those early weeks at Anfield were largely spent plugging leaks, and despite Benítez's trip to Portugal in a bid to curry favour with the Liverpool captain, Chelsea were no longer even bothering with subtleties when it came to their pursuit of Gerrard, with Peter Kenyon openly declaring, 'If he was to become available, then we would definitely be in for Steven Gerrard,' while José Mourinho stiffened the Stamford Bridge stance when saying he would welcome the midfielder with open arms. West London was fluttering its eyelashes quite shamelessly, and the smart money was on Gerrard being attracted by the attention.

A pervading mood of disappointed acceptance over Gerrard's expected departure descended upon the red half of Merseyside, although the mood music about Owen seemed much more positive, with the *Daily Mirror* declaring that a new £65,000-a-week contract was set to be signed by the England striker, while conversely, the *Sunday Express* speculated that he would leave, but only if Gerrard departed for Chelsea, with Benítez reputedly lining up Valencia's Mista as Owen's potential replacement, while Baraja was being mentioned as a surrogate Gerrard. This latter story, of course, was reliant upon Benítez's assertion that he had no intentions of swooping on the players of his former employers being merely a smokescreen.

Within 24 hours of the *Sunday Express* indulging in their latest round of speculation, Gerrard publicly announced his intentions to remain at Liverpool, a decision that he had relayed to a partially surprised Rick Parry on the Saturday. With a sea of microphones thrust toward him, Gerrard was candid about both his decision to stay, and the reasons that had led to him seriously considering leaving, 'I have not really been happy with the progress the club has made over the last two years. For the first time in my career, I seriously thought about the possibility of leaving Liverpool. But after Euro 2004, sitting down with my family, having another meeting with Rick and spending time with my agent, I am staying at Liverpool.'

A delighted and relieved Parry went on to add, 'Stevie said to me, "I can't leave, I've been here since I was eight and I've always wanted to be captain of the club." Never, at any point, did he mention money. It is unusual but fantastic.' Owen, meanwhile, bluntly stated that had Gerrard departed it would have been 'a catastrophe'.

Never far from drama unfolding at Anfield, before June had come to an end Valencia were threatening to sue Benítez over breach of contract, their former employee promising to respond in kind by countersuing over non-payment of salary and bonuses, with a complaint being lodged with the Real Federación Española de Fútbol.

Brinksmanship was clearly not a new experience for Benítez, at least certainly not when it came to his dealings with Valencia.

Into July, and the first week of Benítez's first full month in his new job brought with it the first arrival and departure from the squad he had inherited from Houllier, as Djibril Cissé officially became a Liverpool player when signing from Auxerre for £14.5m in a transfer that had been set up by Benítez's predecessor. Meanwhile, heading toward the exit door, Bruno Cheyrou left for a season-long loan at Olympique de Marseille.

With Liverpool under new management, and Cissé largely viewed as a Houllier signing, there was still much anticipation over where Benítez would cast his net for reinforcements and who he would deem surplus to his requirements. It wasn't long before El Hadji Diouf, Salif Diao, Dietmar Hamann, Milan Baroš, Markus Babbel, Djimi Traoré, and Neil Mellor were all linked to pastures new, while across the weeks in the build-up to the start of pre-season training, Liverpool's interest was being attached to names such as Milan's Fabricio Coloccini, the Málaga defensive midfielder Miguel Ángel, plus another two Valencia mainstays, the Argentine central defender Roberto Ayala and the Spanish international winger Vicente.

As part of this, while the mooted arrivals of Ángel, Ayala, and Vicente were to be well wide of the mark, within a year Diouf, Diao, Babbel, and Baroš would all have departed, and by the summer of 2006 Hamann, Traoré, and Mellor had followed them. Basically, it was easier to identify those who Benítez was likely to move on than it was those he would be looking to bring in. Yet, all the while, the twist in the tail of Owen's future at Liverpool was still very much drifting beneath the radar, and Danny Murphy was not in the Anfield transfer chatter at all.

Onward churned the rumour mill as the *Sunday People* floated the idea that Liverpool were the surprise favourites to sign Patrick Kluivert, the *Daily Mirror* reported links to the Málaga goalkeeper Juan Calatayud in a deal that would have seen Diouf moving in the opposite direction, and the same publication reported an interest from Benítez in the Marseille striker Mido, who would eventually play Premier League football for Tottenham Hotspur, Middlesbrough, Wigan Athletic, and West Ham United. Here we also saw the first rumblings of intent from Real Madrid with regards Owen, as mentioned by the *Daily Express*. By-and-large, it was silly season as far as transfer talk was concerned. It was as if player names were being plucked out of one hat and clubs they might be joining picked from another.

A week prior to Liverpool's first pre-season friendly under Benítez, and one of the players heavily linked with a departure from the club did bid farewell to life at Anfield as Babbel signed for VfB Stuttgart on a free transfer, bringing to an end an association that had been so prosperous during the German international's first season with Liverpool, in 2000/01, as a crucial component of the cup treble side, only to go on to suffer the cruel blow of falling victim to Guillain-Barré syndrome, a rare and debilitating autoimmune condition that left him a shadow of the player he had been upon his eventual return to action.

With a month still to go until the start of the Premier League campaign, Florent Sinama Pongolle was now being linked to a loan move to Saint-Étienne, while the Kluivert stories were promptly ended as he signed for Newcastle United. Next up, Baroš was connected to a switch to Barcelona, having previously been under the scrutiny of Real Madrid, although a £10m valuation by Liverpool was widely viewed as prohibitive to prospective suitors for a player who was was still the Euro 2004 Golden Boot winner.

Meanwhile Diouf, not even allocated a squad number – further underlining Benítez's lack of interest in the player – was attracting the interest of Portsmouth, only to join Bolton Wanderers on a season-long loan a few days later, with Sam Allardyce fending off further competition from Fiorentina and Málaga, while Benítez was now being linked to the former Everton midfielder Oliver Dacourt.

Away from conjecture and hypotheticals, 48 hours before the trip to the Racecourse Ground to face Wrexham, Cissé was finally unveiled at an Anfield press conference during which Benítez stated that he expected Owen to soon sign a new contract. In North Wales, Liverpool were 2-1 winners, with Antony Le Tallec scoring both of Liverpool's goals. Two days later, Benítez and his squad flew off for a three-match tour of the US.

Within days of setting off for Hartford, Liverpool confirmed that they were in talks over the transfer of the Málaga right-back Josemi, who would soon sign on the dotted line as Benítez's first fully autonomous recruit, the player wasting no time in heading Stateside to join up with his new team-mates. A pragmatic rather than showstopping arrival, the rumour mill simply cranked up another gear, with the *Sunday People* reporting interest from Liverpool in Manchester City's Shaun Wright-Phillips.

A 5-1 victory over Celtic at Rentschler Field was the perfect on-pitch start to Liverpool's tour, the goals coming from John Arne Riise, Owen, Henchoz, and a brace for Cissé, with Gerrard and Murphy combining well in midfield as a creative hub. Tempering the good vibes, Šmicer ended the first 45 minutes nursing a knee injury, one which would eventually require surgery, thus ruling him out of Benítez's plans for the next six months. Not ideal for a player with an unenviable track record of injuries, and only one year left on his contract.

At this stage, hopes were still high that Owen's contract situation would be addressed upon Liverpool's return from the US, with Gerrard's commitment to stay being just the reassurance the striker needed to ensure a positive outcome to discussions. One player definitely on the way out, however, was the French midfielder Alou Diarra, who was headed to Lens for a season-long loan, this being a third successive season spent on the road since arriving from Bayern Munich in the summer of 2002.

Diarra's case was a particular oddity, with his move to Lens following on from seasons spent with Le Havre and Bastia. Benítez had elected not to include him in the squad that headed to the States, and at 23, the player was no longer a wet-behind-the-ears prospect. By October 2004 Diarra would be a full French international, and it was perhaps an oversight of the new Liverpool manager not to take a closer look at him; yet with Hamann, Diao, and Igor Bišćan representing a trio of defensive midfielders already ahead of him in the Anfield pecking order, for Diarra to have prospered it would have required the departure of at least one of them, if not two, in the summer of 2004. Diarra's career would progress significantly enough for him to be part of the France squads at the 2006 and 2010 World Cups, as well as for the 2012 European Championship finals.

Liverpool moved on to Toronto and the SkyDome for their next pre-season outing, where they faced the reigning European champions, the now José Mourinho-less Porto, and a 1-0 defeat was absorbed in a game that remained as a stalemate for 85 minutes until Carlos Alberto grabbed the only goal.

Within the slipstream of the Porto game the first hint of Owen unrest began to bubble to the surface, as when pressed on his contract situation he was candid enough to confess, 'We've been speaking for a long time but not since the new manager took charge. No one, including myself, wants this to drag on into the season and hopefully it will be concluded soon,' in a quote that was picked up by all the regular Liverpool beat journalists, to keep the headline writers happy.

Bridging the end of July and the beginning of August, Liverpool related-news remained prominent in the sports pages as the club was granted permission to build a new 60,000-seater stadium in Stanley Park, although the £80m plan was to be referred for scrutiny to John Prescott, the deputy prime minister. Meanwhile, the latest transfer noise focused on Damian Duff playing down talk of a move to Liverpool.

Back on the pitch, Liverpool wound up their pre-season friendlies with a 2-1 victory over Roma at Giants Stadium in East Rutherford. A goal apiece for Cissé and Owen, in either half, cancelled out Marco Delvecchio's opener, and the game also marked the first sighting of Josemi in a Liverpool shirt, appearing as one of half a dozen changes for the start of the second half. Benítez and his team were now just six days away from the first leg of the Champions League third qualifying round first leg away to Graz AK.

Against Roma, Josemi had not been backwards in coming forward when it came to showing the steely side of his game, while Cissé had impressed, not only with his goal but also his pace. Added to this, Hamann had put in 52 compelling minutes when replacing Gerrard and being asked to push forward more than was familiar for him, while Bišćan had done his own cause no harm with a dominant 45 minutes until being replaced by Diao for the second half.

As Liverpool returned to Merseyside, there was much for Benítez to ponder, with confirmation of the seriousness of Šmicer's injury coming and further Anfield departures being agreed: Le Tallec farmed out to Saint-Étienne for what was set to be a year-long loan, and Grégory Vignal heading to Rangers under similar terms.

There had been much expectation surrounding Le Tallec upon his capture by Houllier, along with Sinama Pongolle, from under the nose of Arsène Wenger and Arsenal in 2002, this after the two French teenagers had been star performers at the 2001 FIFA U-17 World Championship in Trinidad and Tobago. Progress had, however, not been swift, and it made perfect sense for Le Tallec to spend a season playing regular football, at a high level and in the land of his birth, although such plans would eventually unravel midway through the campaign.

For Vignal, with only one year remaining on his contract, it was very much a case of what might have been at Liverpool, having impressed at left-back in his early first-team appearances, especially for a spell at the beginning of the 2001/02 season when playing behind the rampaging Riise. For a while, it looked like the perfect combination down the left for Houllier, but fitness and form soon deserted the former Montpellier youth product and a second chance never really materialised as he instead went out on a series of loan spells with Bastia, Rennes, and Espanyol, prior to Ibrox calling.

On the wheeling and dealing went for Benítez as out went Carl Medjani for a season on loan at Lorient, while it came as something of a shock that he accepted a £3m bid from Tottenham Hotspur for Danny Murphy, a player who had been a key element of Houllier's Liverpool, and at 27 still had much to give the club.

In the days that followed, Tottenham's move for Murphy was to break down, and before long Charlton Athletic would take advantage of the situation to gain themselves a £2.5m bargain, this despite reported interest from Everton too. What made the sale of Murphy even more of a surprise, was that he had been one of Liverpool's best performers on the tour of the US. Yet Benítez clearly had other plans in mind.

Suddenly, from a spate of understandable loan deals being agreed, via Murphy and on through to Owen, transfer matters escalated rapidly at Anfield as contract discussions with Liverpool's star striker ground to a halt and much conjecture began to surround his potential non-involvement in the first leg of the Champions League encounter against AK Graz.

Owen's contract talks had been going on for 15 months, and the deadlock had not been broken. News of Murphy's precarious future might well have pushed Owen to look to the exit door too, and *The Independent* were quick to float a £20m price tag for the now unsettled player, citing a potential part-exchange deal for Samuel Eto'o or Fernando Morientes, with Real Madrid's interest growing, this in the wake of their recent failed attempt to sign Thierry Henry.

Five years on from having lost the services of Steve McManaman to Real for free, once again Liverpool were set to see another prized asset depart for the same destination at way below his market value, in a piece of footballing history that would be controversially repeated again over two decades later.

After scoring 158 goals in just under 300 games in a Liverpool shirt, Owen had been too valuable a commodity to allow to wind down his contract to its final year. The situation was a careless one for the club to sleepwalk its way into, and not to tie him into a new deal during the summer, when it – at least from the outside looking in – appeared he was receptive to do so, was to bite hard.

In Austria, Liverpool cruised to a 2-0 victory over Graz, with Gerrard claiming both goals, while Owen struck the image of awkwardness, sat as he was on the bench as an unused substitute as part of a very public kitchen sink drama on an evening that marked Benítez's first competitive game in charge of the club.

On the pitch, Sami Hyypiä came close with an early headed chance that was tipped over the crossbar by Andreas Schranz after a free kick from Steve Finnan. Overall, Schranz was to have a magnificent game in order to keep the scoreline to 2-0, something that would go on to have a knock-on effect for a second leg that would be more nail-biting than it really needed to be.

Graz played well at times, with some excellent short passing and movement, but provided little punch in the final third. Yet there were certainly subtle hints of what they were to be capable of in the second leg, and if anything, Gerrard's opening goal midway through the first half, a fine strike from 25 yards, did more to relax the home side than it did the visitors.

Liverpool and Gerrard's second goal finally arrived 12 minutes from time, after fine work from Cissé, and the captain also had one disallowed midway through the second half when the French striker was adjudged to have committed a foul in the penalty area during the build-up. On a positive night's work from Cissé, he had linked well with Baroš, with both having opportunities to score, Cissé from a right-wing cross-shot and Baroš heading over from eight yards. Schranz was kept busy throughout, pulling off further saves from Hamann, Cissé, and Hyypiä.

With Murphy's move to Charlton now completed, and it seeming like only a matter of time before Owen's departure was going to be confirmed, Liverpool and Benítez were in increasing need of some good news regarding players on the way into the club, only for them to see an £11m bid for Xabi Alonso turned down by Real Sociedad. With three weeks to go before the closure of the summer transfer window, patience was going to be the name of the game when it came to key targets.

While Liverpool had seemingly been circumspect enough not to render Owen cup-tied for the Champions League, Real Madrid had had no such qualms about throwing Fernando Morientes on as a substitute away against Wisła Kraków, replacing Ronaldo for the final 22 minutes with the scoreline lodged at 0-0, from where the Spanish striker went on to find the net twice. José Antonio Camacho, the new Real Madrid head coach, had made no secret of his admiration of Morientes, nor of his reluctance to lose a fine footballer who just happened no longer to fit the *Galácticos* ethos, which was being relentlessly pursued by Florentino Pérez.

This turn of events was a significant blow to Liverpool, and the Owen waters were soon muddied further with Eto'o being ruled out of the transfer equation, the Cameroonian striker forcing through his favoured option of a move to Barcelona with Real Madrid having been keen on him heading to Anfield, as opposed to the Camp Nou and into the possession of their biggest rivals, who would go on to great success across the seasons ahead.

In better news for Benítez, Real Sociedad were becoming increasingly amenable to doing business over Alonso, even going as far as leaving him out of their squad for the pre-season fixture with Osasuna, while rumours of a potential move for Shaun Wright-Phillips were continuing to surface. Amid these manoeuvrings, a hit list of Spanish players was being reputedly drawn up, from which Luis García's name was gaining increasing traction, while rumblings about the teenage duo of the future Spanish international Juanfran and the Málaga left-back Alexis were to come to nothing.

As the endgame of the Owen to Real Madrid saga lurched into view, the true extent of the thin end of the wedge that Liverpool were holding became more and more apparent, with the projected fee having shrunk to around the £8m mark, which was less than half of the number being quoted a fortnight earlier. Added to this, the calibre of any prospective player coming in the opposite direction had diminished, from established frontmen such as Morientes and Eto'o to a relatively unconsidered winger by the name of Antonio Núñez.

On the eve of the start of the new Premier League campaign, Owen was finally unveiled as a Real Madrid player, making for surreal images given he wasn't someone they necessarily required, yet they seemed compelled to add him to their squad in what was a brutal pursuit from a Liverpool perspective.

Owen, with the world at his feet and so much of his career still ahead of him, was never to hit the individual heights he had in a Liverpool shirt again and despite playing on for another nine seasons, he would score only 66 further goals at club level, for Real Madrid, Newcastle United, contentiously Manchester United, and finally Stoke City, as the grass proved not to be quite as green as it had looked elsewhere to him in the summer of 2004.

With a line finally drawn under the Owen situation, much of the money that came in for his signature was swiftly redirected into a £6m bid for García that was readily accepted by Barcelona, with Benítez all set to be reunited with a player who had served him exceptionally well during his year at Real Mallorca, although the transfer would ultimately take a week to iron out.

On a beautifully warm and sunny day in north London, Liverpool began the new Premier League season with a 1-1 draw away to Tottenham Hotspur at White Hart Lane, Jermain Defoe cancelling out a debut strike by Cissé on a day when Jamie Carragher was deployed in central defence alongside Sami Hyypiä, while Steve Finnan was pushed up on the right-hand side of midfield with Josemi slotting in at right-back.

It was an afternoon that represented wider change at White Hart Lane – Jacques Santini was making his bow as Tottenham's new head coach, a position he would relinquish before Christmas, and the former French national manager couldn't have complained had he started his short reign with a defeat given that Gerrard should have had a first-half penalty when pulled back after twisting and turning away from Phil Ifil.

With Owen no longer a Liverpool player, it was a soothing sight to see Cissé open the scoring after 38 minutes via a Carragher header and Finnan cross, while Defoe's 71st-minute equaliser came against the run of play, and while one point gained at Tottenham on the opening day could be viewed as a positive outcome it was also a case of mulling over what might have been the full three points too.

Liverpool's travelling supporters were in fine voice: not having been able to bid Houllier farewell back in May, a banner in the away section reading simply 'Merci Gérard' was unfurled, the man himself being present at the game in a new capacity working as an analyst for the French TV coverage. Undoubtedly the tribute, along with the goal for Cissé, will have pleased him immeasurably.

Three days later, Liverpool reached a preliminary agreement with Real Sociedad for the signing of Alonso, the two clubs settling on a fee of £10.7m; with Alonso's agent Iñaki Ibanez insisting the deal was done and that Real Madrid were out of the reckoning, it was a much-needed piece of good news for Benítez with regards to his rebuilding plans.

With two weeks to go before the transfer window was to close, there was still plenty of scope for arrivals and departures at Anfield and Tottenham were now showing an interest in Finnan, who was under threat from Josemi at right-back, while Núñez was expected to contest the right-hand side of midfield, theoretically limiting the Ireland international's opportunities further. Also, Hamann's future remained in doubt and a hot topic of conjecture.

A day beyond news of the progression in Alonso's projected signing, Núñez was unveiled at Anfield but in his very first training session he partially tore a medial knee ligament, twisting the joint when nobody was near him. It was a freak injury and a massive setback for the player, and for Benítez, the blow leaving Núñez to play catch-up from the word go, his first-team debut not coming until late November.

As Liverpool's first home game of the season loomed, with the visit of Kevin Keegan's Manchester City just 24 hours away, the pivotal signings of Alonso and García were finally completed and the poor football on display during the first half of the following day's game simply accentuated the need for their involvement as soon as possible.

With Keegan's side quick to close down Liverpool's players when they were in possession of the ball, the first half ended with Nicolas Anelka haunting the team he had wanted to sign permanently for in the summer of 2002 when snatching the opening goal. With potential for frustration ahead in the second half, it was a relief when

Baroš netted the equaliser just three minutes beyond the restart, and having set that goal up it was Gerrard who claimed the winner on an afternoon when Richard Dunne was sent off in the latter stages for a second bookable offence, provoking much rancour.

Next up for Liverpool was the perceived formality of the second leg of the Champions League third qualifying round, and the visit to Anfield of AK Graz. In the build-up, Hyypiä was in bullish mood regarding his team's hopes and aspirations in the competition for 2004/05, as *The Independent* picked up on his thoughts, 'Three years ago this club was in the quarter-finals of the Champions League and I do not see any reason we can't do that again, at least,' while Benítez went on to say, 'We must win this match because the fans want us to go to the semi-final, even the final, of the Champions League.'

Confidence was clearly high on the eve of the game but it was greatly misplaced as Liverpool were almost undone in the most embarrassing fashion, slipping to an unimpressive 1-0 defeat to their Austrian guests, grimly hanging on at the end to progress to the group stage 2-1 on aggregate, on an evening when starts were handed to Henchoz, Diao, and Darren Potter, while Stephen Warnock appeared for the last half an hour, replacing Harry Kewell.

Croatian international Mario Tokić scored the only goal to leverage an entirely unnecessary sense of peril upon Anfield, and the only solace that Benítez, his team, and those supporters who had filed through the turnstiles could take from the night was that the final whistle had been reached, and a place in the group stage had been attained.

It had been an undeniably nervous evening at Anfield: Benítez's players had far too often given possession away and were regularly second best in their efforts at picking up the second ball. It had been a game that had posed more questions than answers, yet a path all the way to Istanbul could now be traversed.

Chapter Four

What Do You Want from Me?
It's Not How It Used to Be

UEFA WOULD have been relieved that Liverpool limped over the finish line and into the group stage of the 2004/05 Champions League, as AK Graz should have ended their game at Anfield with ten men after the Spanish referee Luis Medina Cantalejo flashed a second yellow card at midfielder René Aufhauser in the 77th minute, without thinking to brandish an accompanying red to go with it.

A potential diplomatic incident averted, the draw pitted Liverpool alongside Monaco, Olympiacos, and Deportivo de La Coruña in Group A. Monaco had been the beaten finalists in 2004, Deportivo had lost to eventual winners Porto in the semi-finals, while Olympiakos were no strangers to the group stages of the tournament. Rafael Benítez had much to unpack.

With August not yet behind the new manager, and with Djimi Traoré on the brink of moving to Everton for £1.5m, Benítez was at pains to persuade him to stay in what would be the last transfer- or non-transfer-related activity of the summer window at Anfield. In terms of David Moores and Rick Parry's attempts to bring more investment into the club, the Redrow building magnate Steve Morgan admitted defeat in his second and final attempt to buy a major shareholding.

Liverpool now headed to Bolton Wanderers, where Benítez was to experience pitting his wits against Sam Allardyce for the first time, but the boost of being able to hand Xabi Alonso and Luis García their debuts was offset by a numbing 1-0 defeat and a first Premier League loss of the season. On the back of losing at home to Graz, these were to represent early indicators of the inconsistencies to come for Liverpool, although what should have been a late equaliser from García was incorrectly ruled out as offside.

On a forgettable afternoon, Sami Hyypiä had to be withdrawn after only 14 minutes due to a broken nose sustained in a challenge with the robust Kevin Davies, who would then go on to score the only goal of the game. Again, struggling with picking up the second ball, the loss of Hyypiä's aerial presence was a blow, and his replacement Traoré was given a tough time.

With Stephen Warnock handed a start to add an extra figure in central midfield, Djibril Cissé dropped down to the bench until being introduced at the start of the second half on an afternoon that was something of a culture shock for Alonso and García, and Steven Gerrard was shadowed by Ivan Campo throughout; with Dietmar Hamann sitting in front of the back four, it left a lot of the creative responsibility on a trio of players that had either no or next to no Premier League experience going into this game with Harry Kewell and Florent Sinama Pongolle also missing through injury.

While there is never a good time for a defeat, it is particularly frustrating to absorb one before an international break presents itself, thus leaving a two-week gap during which to lick club wounds, but they were to bounce back impressively on the resumption of Premier League action when they took West Bromwich Albion apart at Anfield with García the star turn in a fluid and stylish team performance. Alonso appeared as a second-half substitute, and the crowd filed away at full time with a spring in their stride and a buzz in the air.

Gerrard had opened the scoring in the 16th minute and sent García on his way to dispatch Liverpool's third on the hour, with Steve Finnan having netted his first goal for the club a few minutes before the interval, and the collective performance was one of great substance: the best so far of Benítez's reign.

With Cissé nominally named as the lone striker, this was far from a formation with only one up front as García and Kewell were swift to offer support, making for a front three whenever Liverpool were on the attack, West Brom dropping back with two deep lines of four and five, only for Gerrard's relatively early goal to render Gary Megson's overt pragmatism a moot point almost from the off.

Bolton and West Brom offered two differing versions of meat and potato football in those games, with the defeat to Allardyce's version having been an eighth win for the Trotters in their last ten Premier League outings, straddling the end of 2003/04 and the beginning of 2004/05, and it lifted them into third place, while Benítez's success over Megson was gleaned from a newly promoted team that had yet to register a win upon their return to the top flight, a club where conflict between manager and chairman would lead to a parting of the ways the following month.

Set against this, Liverpool's performance against West Brom was of such an upbeat nature that it would have been difficult for any team to have lived with them that afternoon, whereas against Bolton, while distinctly second-best for much of the game, Benítez and his players should have come away with a point. As ever with football, you can only win, lose, or draw against what's in front of you, and just when you play a team has a huge influence on proceedings, as West Brom would go on to pull off a great escape act from impending relegation at the season's end while from late October to early January Bolton would fail to register a league win at all, inclusive of losing all of their December fixtures, before rallying again in the new year. Timing is everything.

So, with caveats at play, since the defeat at home to Graz, domestically it had been one step back and one step forward in the build-up to the visit of Monaco. Although Monaco were less than four months on from their flirtation with European club football's biggest prize, through a combination of transfers, loans ending and injuries their line-up at Anfield on Group A's opening night had only five survivors from their starting 11 for the loss to José Mourinho's Porto.

Ludovic Giuly had been sold to Barcelona, Jérôme Rothen had been seduced by the attention of his boyhood favourites Paris Saint-Germain, where he joined the returning loanee Édouard Cissé, Fernando Morientes was back at Real Madrid, Dado Pršo had moved on to Rangers, while Hugo Ibarra had gone back to his mother club, Porto. At Anfield, it was a heavily restructured team that was named by their head coach Didier Deschamps, even finding himself deprived of the services of the suspended newcomer Javier Saviola.

The two teams had experienced similar starts to their respective domestic campaigns: just like Liverpool, Monaco had been faultless at home, but inconsistent on the road during those early weeks of the new season as they adjusted to the absorbing of their new arrivals, not only Saviola, but also Maicon, Diego Pérez, François Modesto, Mohamed Kallon, Pontus Farnerud, and Javier Chevantón.

So, on the opening night of the Champions League, Monaco's visit to Anfield offered an intriguing test for Benítez and his new set of players, especially against opponents that still had the majority of their Champions League Final defence intact, inclusive of Patrice Evra, Gaël Givet, and Julien Rodriguez, while they could boast the midfield combativeness and organisational abilities of Akis Zikos, and the esoteric attacking stylings of Emmanuel Adebayor. Liverpool and Monaco undoubtedly had teams packed with talent, but both were very much in stages of transition.

With Gérard Houllier in attendance at Anfield, as were the old coaching guard of Phil Thompson and Sammy Lee, alongside a cast list as long as your arm of other Liverpool European Cup winners of the club's glittering past, it was to prove a relatively routine win for Benítez's side, which tied in perfectly to Liverpool's fine home form and Monaco's issues on the road with Deschamps's club having now won only three of their 20 away games of the Champions League era, Liverpool conversely never having lost at home to opponents from Ligue 1.

Cissé opened the scoring midway through the first half, with his 68th-minute replacement Milan Baroš adding the second goal seven minutes from time. Together, the two had struggled to gel as a partnership during the early exchanges of this post-Michael Owen new world order of Liverpool's, but independently of one another they made the most crucial of contributions, on an evening when a goalless draw between Deportivo de La Coruña and Olympiacos at the Estadio Riazor had meant Benítez and his players were out of the Group A blocks as the early pace-setters.

On an evening when Benítez's three available Spanish acquisitions shone, García was all skill and deftness, Alonso was dynamic in his work alongside the metronomic Gerrard, while Josemi was defensive solidity personified at right-back and also provided the assist for Baroš's goal. A fine collective performance by all involved, and had it not been for the agility of Monaco goalkeeper Flavio Roma, Liverpool's winning margin would have wider, and they wouldn't have had to bide their time until the 83rd minute to obtain the cushion of a two-goal advantage – this on a night when Jerzy Dudek was largely unoccupied.

Shrugging off an initially tentative start, it was via a well-worked free-kick routine by Gerrard and García that the ball was met by the delayed run of Cissé, who dispatched it for the opening goal with power and precision. Before the interval, García was twice denied by the reactions of Roma.

Shortly before the hour, Cissé should have doubled the lead when sent through on Roma by a flicked header from Kewell, only to hit the goalkeeper rather than the back of the net, and it was eventually down to Baroš to settle any stirring nerves, side-footing home after chesting the ball down from Josemi's long pass, before winding a way past Roma, and Sébastien Squillaci.

A consummate start to Liverpool's Champions League campaign, the threat of Monaco had been nullified to such an impressive extent that they were funnelled into aiming a succession of formulaic high balls into Dudek's penalty area in a bid to utilise the height of Adebayor, while Maicon was pushed higher up the right to test the defensive resolve of John Arne Riise. Monaco's best spell came early in the second half with the score at 1-0, making the belated nature of Liverpool's second goal a vague concern.

For Benítez, the conundrum was all about fitting Alonso into his midfield alongside Gerrard. Finnan had been deployed on the right of midfield once again, while Hamann had dropped down to the bench to enable the Gerrard and Alonso partnership, meaning that García played centrally, in a roaming remit in front of the midfield, slotting in behind Cissé.

Benítez opted for a 4-4-1-1 formation, up against Monaco's cautious 3-1-4-2, and Deschamps fielded three central defenders in Squillaci, Givet and the withdrawn Zikos, before throwing on Souleymane Camara in place of Evra for the second half, to offer Adebayor more support. In *The Times* Deschamps conceded, 'We got what we deserved … Our goalkeeper saved us from even worse problems.'

Benítez also said in *The Times*, 'Normally when you win you are satisfied but if you see your team win while creating so many chances, then it is even more pleasing. Always you can do things better, but we played well, we won, we scored goals, so it is a fantastic start. Tonight is a short step forward, no more.' He was clearly delighted with his team's performance but he was in no mood to get carried away.

In *The Times*'s coverage the following day, Gerrard went on to say, 'It's always important to win your home games, especially in a group situation. They made it difficult for us, but we worked hard, played well and scored two goals. We limited them to a few chances on goal, which is pleasing. They had a little bit of joy for a spell in the second half, so it was important to get the second goal to kill them off, especially in the Champions League because you're up against such quality.'

Meanwhile, at the Riazor, Deportivo had been left frustrated by a belligerent and resolute Olympiacos rearguard, shorn as they were of wider creativity, due an injury to Víctor Sánchez and forced to field a heavily restructured midfield due to the further absences of Mauro Silva and Aldo Duscher.

It had been an ideal start to life in Group A for Liverpool, and next up in the Champions League it would be a trip to Athens to take on Olympiacos, opponents they had defeated in the Greek capital en route to winning the UEFA Cup in 2000/01. There was every reason for optimism that another positive result could be picked up this time around.

Chapter Five

Olympian Spirits

FIVE DAYS beyond their win over Monaco, Liverpool were at Old Trafford for a Monday night assignment against bitter rivals Manchester United, neither side having made a convincing start to their Premier League campaign.

Even though they sat tenth going into the game, Liverpool were three places above Sir Alex Ferguson's team at kick-off time having played one game fewer, thus making what was traditionally English football's biggest fixture an early season mid-table bunfight, albeit one that was enlivened by not only the usual electrical charge that pulsates through it but also the pantomime provided by the return to action of Rio Ferdinand, fresh from having served the full extent of his eight-month ban for missing a random doping test, plus a calamitous injury to Steven Gerrard that would put him out of action for the next two months.

On an evening when anything that could go wrong for Liverpool did go wrong, Gerrard was forced to withdraw six minutes before the interval, the latest victim in an increasing line of England internationals to suffer a broken metatarsal – a blow that would result in him missing not only the impending trip to Olympiacos in the Champions League and the back-to-back encounters with Deportivo de La Coruña but also the Premier League visit to Stamford Bridge to face Chelsea and a duo of World Cup qualifiers against Wales and Azerbaijan.

A chastening night collectively, in a theme of it's not my party and I'll cry if I want to, Cristiano Ronaldo's response to not being the pre-match centre of attention was to spend his evening tormenting John Arne Riise, the Portuguese global phenomenon-in-the-making proving the home team's inspiration of a first half in which Liverpool were left reeling. Ronaldo struck the post from 25 yards and Ruud van Nistelrooy forced Jerzy Dudek into a smart save before they finally made what seemed an inevitable breakthrough.

Two headed goals, one in either half, from Mikaël Silvestre sealed the points – a man Gérard Houllier, just as with Ronaldo, had made efforts to sign before he moved to Old Trafford – it was here that rumblings of disapproval over zonal marking began to be aired by professional football watchers. Yet, just like the loss at Bolton, there were caveats at play with the second of Manchester United's two goals coming via a corner that should not have been awarded, while for a ten-minute spell at 1-1 Liverpool looked the more likely team to go on to claim the win. With Gerrard's injury added into the mix, fortune was once again not favouring Rafael Benítez.

One step back at Old Trafford, it was one step forward five days later at Anfield when Liverpool brushed

Norwich City aside, cruising to a third Premier League win out of three on home soil. A game played out upon a backdrop of more takeover speculation, this time the emerging stories surrounded the Walton-born filmmaker Mike Jeffries and his business partner Stuart Ford, who were fronting the Kraft family backed L4 consortium in a flirtation that would eventually fizzle out in January.

It was with a dominant display that Liverpool ran out 3-0 winners, and in the absence of Gerrard, Xabi Alonso was deployed as a roving playmaker, sometimes dropping deep, often advancing forward, pinging an array of penetrative short and long passes, moving with fluidity, distributing the ball with an unerring precision, all the while protected by the unruffled Dietmar Hamann, supported further still by the inclusion of Stephen Warnock.

Up front, caution was thrown to the wind, with Djibril Cissé and Milan Baroš starting and Luis García offering extra attacking impetus, at least nominally on the right. It was a fast start that Liverpool made, finding themselves two goals to the good within 26 minutes thanks to Baroš and García and reaching the interval with a 2-0 lead that could easily have been doubled, García having hit Robert Green's post and Cissé almost being gifted a goal by a generously chaotic Norwich defence.

Denied in the first half, Cissé did eventually get the goal his efforts deserved midway through the second period, a goal that acted as the cue for Benítez to withdraw not only the scorer but Alonso too in the name of conserving energy for the midweek trip to

Athens, although he did allow García to complete the full 90 minutes on an afternoon when he was a blizzard of skill and always a danger to the Norwich defence, often drifting into central areas, operating behind Cissé and Baroš to create a triumvirate that the visitors couldn't cope with.

Against an effervescent performance and arguably the best Liverpool had yet played under the guidance of Benítez, Norwich had been exceptionally benevolent in repeatedly handing over possession of the ball then backing off, inviting their opponents on. On one hand, just like with West Bromwich Albion, it was another newly promoted team that Liverpool had artistically dismantled, but as part of a wider theme they had still won all of their home fixtures, apart from that unnecessarily uncomfortable night against AK Graz. However they were still to win away from Anfield, and next up was a double-header on the road, firstly to Athens and then to Chelsea.

Armed with the option of Harry Kewell, back from the thigh injury that had kept him out of the Norwich game, for the trip to Athens Benítez could also once again call upon Josemi, with Steve Finnan again pushing up on to the right of midfield, while Warnock retained his place in the starting line-up and Cissé dropped down to the bench in order for Baroš to be deployed as the lone forward.

Affording the traditionally hostile welcome to Liverpool at the newly upgraded Karaiskakis Stadium, Olympiacos's supporters brought vibrancy, colour, noise, passion, aggression, and their pluming red pyros to the party, and their heroes on the pitch responded nothing but positively to the mood music while the visitors floundered.

Undone by a 32-year-old Brazilian with questionable knees, who was left insulted by Celtic, frustrated by Bolton Wanderers, and snubbed entirely by Liverpool in the summer, this was very much the Rivaldo Show, a window of redemption and a middle finger brandished in the faces of all who had doubted he could turn back the clock to his glory days, his World Cup winner's medal having been collected what felt like an eternity ago rather than just two years since, and his most recent experience of football in Europe having been an unsatisfactory spell at Milan.

Every time Rivaldo swung a corner or a free kick into the Liverpool penalty area it caused consternation to their bedraggled defence, and that Olympiacos only won by such a narrow margin was something of a mystery on a night when a hopelessly isolated Baroš could make little headway at the other end of the pitch.

Ieroklis Stoltidis scored the game's only goal, a 17th-minute header, the ball arriving to him from a Rivaldo free kick, finding him in far too much space within the penalty area, once again exposing Benítez's zonal defensive system to critical scrutiny. Olympiacos could have scored long before even that relatively early goal, Giannis Okkas hitting Dudek's left-hand post after only five minutes when played in by Stoltidis. Okkas would later strike the Liverpool crossbar with a header from a Rivaldo corner.

This Liverpool performance was a shuddering reminder of so many of those stilted afternoons and evenings at the tail end of the Houllier era, where defensive vulnerabilities were offset only by a lack of a cutting edge up front, and on this occasion – despite a red card being brandished at Anastasios Pantos with six minutes remaining – as even with a late one-man advantage, Benítez's side still couldn't make an attacking impression despite the introduction of Kewell immediately after the interval, and the addition of an extra striker in Cissé for the final 17 minutes.

While the loss of Gerrard's drive in midfield had clearly been an issue in Athens, an engine room containing Alonso and Hamann should have been capable of both vision and discipline, flanked as it was by Finnan to the right and Warnock to the left, Kewell then replacing Warnock from the bench, yet a lack of boldness from Benítez in fielding Baroš on his own up front proved costly, with García suffering a frustrating evening as the projected link between midfield and attack.

Not even at the races during the first half, Liverpool did at least inject a little more aggression in the second period, yet they were wildly unrecognisable as the team that had dismantled Norwich a few days earlier, a schism between the home and away versions of Benítez's side becoming increasingly obvious.

Ultimately it was a quiet night in goal for Antonis Nikopolidis, Olympiacos's 2004 European Championship-winning goalkeeper – not one single effort from the visitors on target – with Liverpool getting their approach badly wrong, and perhaps giving the opposition too much respect. On one hand here was a team that had lost on home soil only three times across the previous eight years, inhabited not only by Brazilians of high repute – Rivaldo's presence complimented by his compatriot and former Barcelona team-mate Giovanni – but also a quartet of players that had been part of Greece's magnificently unlikely glory in the Euros less than three months earlier.

Conversely, despite Olympiacos and Greek football in general enjoying an unprecedented spring in its stride, with Liverpool having already impressively beaten Monaco in their opening group game, here had been a golden opportunity for Liverpool to strengthen their position at the top of Group A with the still-new boss Benítez next facing home and away Champions League fixtures against the familiar foes of Deportivo de La Coruña.

When scratching around for positives from an unforgiving night in Athens, Finnan had put in another fine performance to impress Benítez, this after the Spaniard had toyed with the idea of selling the Ireland international after his recruitment of Josemi, while collectively, the endeavour shown in the second half had been an improvement on the abject first 45. That said, it couldn't have been much worse.

Elsewhere, Monaco bounced back from their loss at Anfield by procuring a 2-0 victory of their own at the Stade Louis II against Deportivo de La Coruña thanks to goals from Mohamed Kallon and Javier Saviola. It was a combination of results that left Liverpool in second place in Group A, a point behind Olympiacos and ahead of Monaco on goal difference.

Meanwhile, off the pitch, Tony Blair's Labour government had just given their approval for the building of Liverpool's long-proposed new 60,000-seater stadium on Stanley Park. After much agonising over whether to rebuild Anfield or to move to a new-build stadium, a prospect initially mooted in the mid-1960s, through the drive of Rick Parry a decision had finally, seemingly, been made in the summer of 2002 to break ground some 500 yards or so from what had been the Reds' home ever since their 1892 formation.

A polarising option – more people than would be comfortable to now admit so were in favour of the move – this was a design of stadium that looked no better than a larger version of Bolton Wanderers' relatively new home. Initially earmarked to be completed in time for the start of the 2005/06 season, at a cost of £60-70m, the original plan had been to build to a capacity of 70,000 at a projected cost of £120m, only to see that scheme reduced to a 55,000 capacity that would have scope for further extension.

Arguments reigned. Given that the 2002 version of Anfield had a capacity that rested at just under 10,000 less than a prospective New Anfield of 55,000, those who were defiantly against cashing in the ancestral homestead were aghast at the concept of sending in the bulldozers in the name of a Meccano build that was less than the 57,000 capacity feasibility studies had purportedly suggested the existing stadium could be stretched to via expansion. There were even rumours about blueprints of an expanded Anfield Road end, dating back to the 1990s, which was reputedly the favoured option of chairman David Moores.

By the autumn of 2004, the red tape involved had meant nothing more than tentative groundwork had taken place, and the cost of materials had risen exponentially. Funding had become a sticking point and Moores and Parry were exploring all avenues of potential incoming investment, a saga that would eventually lead to Liverpool falling into the hands of Tom Hicks and George Gillett, who would rip the 2004 stadium plans up before going on to take the club to the very brink of administration by 2011, via the release of another new set of plans in 2007.

Back in 2004, however, this was all still unwittingly over the horizon, and the thoughts of Liverpool supporters were predominantly focused upon challenging for honours, albeit upon a landscape where the club was undeniably falling behind its rivals, both on and off the pitch, with Manchester United representing the bogeyman, Arsenal's Invincibles just two years away from their own stadium move, and Chelsea's rouble revolution seeing them disappear over the horizon too.

On multiple fronts, there was hard work ahead for Liverpool.

Chapter Six

Crown Court

SINCE THE loss to Olympiacos, Liverpool had made two trips to west London which straddled the October international break. A narrow defeat had been sustained at Chelsea, while a mad 4-2 victory at Fulham had been picked up for a first away win of the Rafael Benítez era. Travel sickness, and with continued issues in adapting to zonal marking for Liverpool – Olympiacos's winning goal had been the fifth from the last seven conceded by Benítez's team to stem from a set piece – questions were being raised as the trip to Chelsea loomed. At Stamford Bridge, Chris Kirkland replaced Jerzy Dudek in goal and put in a solid performance, while Jamie Carragher was excellent in central defence alongside Sami Hyypiä, yet Josemi was regularly exposed to the speed and skill of Damian Duff, the Irishman who had been perpetually linked with a move to Liverpool during the Houllier era and continued to be so during the summer of 2004.

Fielding an adventurous line-up, Benítez opted for a theoretical boldness that had been absent in Athens, deploying Djimi Traoré at left-back and Salif Diao as his defensive midfielder rather than Dietmar Hamann, a double dose of pragmatism that allowed John Arne Riise to push up on to the left of midfield with Luis García operating down the right, Xabi Alonso in the playmaking role, Harry Kewell handed the freedom of being the central link between midfield and attack, and Djibril Cissé usurping Milan Baroš for the sole striker's position.

Yes, it was a bold approach, yet it was also an unbalanced one, with García unable to offer much protection to Josemi from Duff while the effervescence of Joe Cole gave Diao a flurry of headaches. The seemingly close 1-0 scoreline owed much to the profligacy of an out-of-sorts Frank Lampard, who squandered a trio of decent chances, while Liverpool's best two openings were presented to and wasted by Cissé, and although Baroš was thrown into the mix in the 71st minute significant efforts at goal were only marginally better than they had been in Athens.

Defeat at Stamford Bridge left Liverpool down in 11th position, 12 points behind leaders Arsenal and just five points clear of the relegation zone, the difference between Benítez's team at Anfield and on the road being just as stark as it gets. On home soil there was light aplenty, yet on their travels Liverpool were encountering only darkness.

Beyond the international break, at Craven Cottage another step backwards had looked all too likely when despite being the brighter of the two teams during the early exchanges, Liverpool found themselves trailing 2-0 at half-time. Luís Boa Morte struck twice within six minutes up to the half-hour mark for Fulham, and even

Zat Knight's own goal five minutes after the interval appeared to be a gift that the visitors were not going to be capable of building on.

Erring on over-caution with Alonso, fresh from his international travel exertions with Spain, and with an eye on the visit to Anfield of Deportivo, Benítez was already without the services of Steve Finnan, who was suffering with a stomach upset. In a game that fluctuated wildly, Baroš's 71st-minute equaliser was the first effort on target by a player in red yet it lit the touchpaper on a stunning finish to the game, with Liverpool finding themselves down to ten men six minutes later only to take the lead two minutes beyond Josemi's sending off for picking up a second yellow card after a foul on Boa Morte.

A curled and subtly deflected free kick from Alonso put Liverpool ahead before a startled-looking Igor Bišćan settled matters with a piledriver from distance in injury time, just seconds after being introduced from the bench, provoking bedlam in the away section. It was an affirming moment for those who were there. Here was a Liverpool that suffered mood swings, offering sweet and sour moments almost in equal measure, but it did look like the man on the touchline, animatedly conducting matters, appeared to be armed with a plan of some sort. This was a football team that was learning to ride its bike all over again, and on a game-to-game basis it was anyone's guess whether they would fall off or nail the wheelie and bunny hop.

Still no Steven Gerrard, and with Alonso among the substitutes rather than in the starting line-up, a central midfield pairing of Hamann and Diao made for little in the way of expansion and imagination in the engine room. After the Senegalese international had been consistently bested by Mark Pembridge during the first 45 minutes, Benítez replaced him with Alonso for the beginning of the second half, an alteration that the home side's former Everton midfielder simply couldn't cope with and also resulted in neutering the first half effectiveness of Steed Malbranque.

Incredibly, this was the first time that Liverpool had overturned a half-time deficit away from home to win a league game for 13 years. Alonso's studious approach to the game made all the difference after the interval, his vision and calm authority inspiring those around him to greater things than they had managed in the first half.

In time, Alonso would take to life on Merseyside with great verve, on and off the pitch, although he was initially disgruntled that he couldn't get Sky Sports up and running so as to be able to keep a watchful eye on Spanish football. A habitual notetaker, the tactical and future coaching mind was clear to see even when still only aged 22; he was considered enough to spend time during the build-up to Deportivo's visit to Anfield talking to several of their players in order to gauge the levels of intent and how their confidence was holding from their position at the bottom of Group A, with just one point obtained from their first two fixtures.

Real Madrid and Manchester United had been put off Real Sociedad's £10.7m asking price for Alonso, but Benítez's eager willingness on paying the fee was already looking a shrewd decision. It certainly hadn't taken long for chatter over the cost to dissipate, with Alonso's obvious quality soon making him the envy of every club across Europe.

Even more so now, given Gerrard's absence, there was great interest in Alonso, García, and Josemi going up against Spanish opposition in a Liverpool shirt for the first time, Deportivo being the first team that Alonso had scored a competitive senior goal against. That said, he had never been on the winning side against Javier Irureta's team despite having faced them on seven occasions in Real Sociedad colours.

Deportivo had been Primera División champions in 1999/2000, and Champions League regulars as well as semi-finalists in 2003/04, with an added Copa del Rey being won in 2002. One of Spanish football's heavier hitters for over a decade, their metronomic consistency over that period of time had seen them obtain top-three finishes for nine of the previous 12 seasons domestically, and their performances should have yielded more honours throughout the 1990s and early 2000s than the one league title, two Copa del Rey triumphs and one Supercopa de España.

By 2004/05, Deportivo had unwittingly begun to regress, and they were now heavily reliant upon the man-marking talents of Mauro Silva, the 36-year-old Brazilian, while their creativity was supplied by the wonderful Juan Carlos Valerón, with Víctor Sánchez providing the threat from wide, someone Benítez had been linked with prior to the transfer window closing. Up front, Deportivo could call upon the Spanish internationals Diego Tristán, Albert Luque, and Pedro Munitis, plus the Uruguayan international Walter Pandiani.

Still with strength in all departments, Deportivo could depend upon the former Spanish international goalkeeper José Molina behind a defence populated by more internationals in the shapes of Manuel Pablo, César Martín, Jorge Andrade, and Joan Capdevila, while there was a strong Argentine flavour supplied by Lionel Scaloni, Aldo Duscher, and the recent addition, Fabricio Coloccini – the last of this trio having been considered yet passed upon by Benítez during the summer.

As inconsistent as Liverpool had been domestically so far, Deportivo were languishing in eighth in the Primera División when they made the trip to Anfield, and stunningly, despite their role as the top seeds in Group A, they would fail to score a single goal during their six group games. The watching La Coruña public were soon to become disillusioned with the increasingly conservative stylings of Javier Irureta, the title-winning head coach.

Going into the game, Alonso feared that Deportivo would attempt to retain possession of the ball and aim to slow the tempo down. After a disjointed start to their own campaign, inclusive of losing at home to Osasuna and Valencia – the latter defeat involving shipping five goals – they had recently won away at Real Madrid by employing such strangulation tactics.

It was a style of football that was palatable while the team was successful, but with results beginning to ebb there would be a very different reaction, and Irureta would depart the club at the end of the season; however, without him, Deportivo would never be the same force again. Then again, nor would Irureta achieve much away from the Estadio Riazor, with short and unsatisfying spells in charge of Real Betis and Real Zaragoza. This was Deportivo's fifth successive season of Champions League football and it would also be their last to date.

Alonso's pre-match fears were to be well-founded as Deportivo spun a night of frustration for Benítez and Liverpool, the visitors keeping to their compact shape and disciplined adherence to an austere game plan, while the home side lacked a cutting edge.

This was Kirkland's first Champions League outing of the season, after the dropping of Dudek following his indecisiveness in Athens. In front of Kirkland, Hyypiä and Carragher continued as the central defensive pairing, while Josemi was again deployed at right-back and Traoré was once more at left-back, with Riise continuing on the left of midfield.

García was moved to the right, the recovered Finnan sat among the substitutes, while Alonso and Hamann were paired from the start in central midfield after the unsuccessful Diao experiments at Stamford Bridge and Craven Cottage. This meant that Cissé was partnered up front with Baroš as Kewell was restricted to a place on the bench, having missed the win at Fulham on the back of having played behind Cissé at Chelsea.

Despite Benítez deploying two strikers, Cissé and Baroš again struggled to gel, and while Liverpool created chances and the manager was bold enough to suggest this had been the best he'd seen of his team so far, it was the aggression of Deportivo's defending that ensured the result was manhandled toward a goalless draw.

After a bright start from Liverpool, where a goal at that stage could have led to a very different evening, they slowly ran out of ideas during a second half in which Valerón might have punished their profligacy on the hour when failing to take advantage of defensive indecision and a fine cross from Víctor.

Earlier in the game, Riise had cleared a César Martín header off the line, but Deportivo were restricted to just these two opportunities while Alonso was again at the hub of Liverpool's best football, and it was he who had their best chance of the game, forcing Molina into a smart 34th-minute save. Perpetually unbalanced by Liverpool's movement, beyond Alonso's effort Deportivo were reliant upon a further trio of fine saves by Molina, two from Cissé, one from García, plus two crucial tackles by Manuel Pablo, again denying Cissé and the tireless Baroš.

As the game rolled through its last 25 minutes, Benítez rearranged the chairs with Kewell representing a straight swap for Riise on 66 minutes and ten minutes later Finnan replaced Cissé, much to the French international's displeasure, throwing a bottle of water from the bench in frustration and to the bemusement of those around him.

Finnan slotted in on the right of midfield with García switching to a central role behind Baroš, until he too was withdrawn in favour of Florent Sinama Pongolle for the last few minutes, and these constituted changes that almost worked as Kewell came close with a stoppage-time free kick. It wasn't to be, the result at least meaning that Liverpool maintained second place in Group A on goal difference, with Monaco crafting themselves a 2-1 victory over Olympiacos and Javier Saviola again starring for Didier Deschamps's team.

Pongolle's involvement in the game, no matter for how short a run he was handed, had made for an intriguing bookend to pre-match stories intimating that he had handed in a transfer request, information that seemed to be a complete surprise to Benítez when it was put to him as a question in the build-up.

Frustration undeniable in not being able to conjure up a winning goal, Liverpool still had much to be positive about from their performance with Alonso's fine display in midfield being supplemented by a commanding central defensive masterclass by Carragher, who kept Valerón quiet all night.

On an evening when Liverpool couldn't make the breakthrough in their game, almost goadingly, Michael Owen was scoring the only goal for Real Madrid against Dynamo Kyiv, his first for his new club, yet Benítez was still bullish despite the dropping of two crucial points. 'If we play like we did today, we can win away and at home I'm sure,' he claimed in *The Times*, going on to say, 'I'm not happy with the result, but I'm very happy with the way we played.'

Halfway through the group stage, Liverpool had won one, drawn one, and lost one, failing to build upon their opening-night win against the new group leaders.

Worryingly for Benítez, although their easiest game on paper would be the group-ending evening at home to Olympiacos, before they were to get there, potential Champions League-ending trips to La Coruña and Monte Carlo were to come.

At this point it meant there was no guarantee that Liverpool would still have a place in the knockout round to play for by the time that the Greek champions were due to roll into Anfield. At that point they trailed Olympiacos on the head-to-head rule, with both teams on four points, two behind Monaco, and two ahead of Deportivo.

With little time to consider the permutations, Liverpool wouldn't have long to wait for their return against Deportivo: only 15 days separated the fixtures, the second one where defeat needed to be avoided at all costs.

Chapter Seven

It's Eye-gor. Not Eee-gor

SIGNIFICANT BODY blows had been sustained since the start of the season by Liverpool but confidence was gradually growing, especially through Xabi Alonso's increasing influence. He would provide crucial assists in the Premier League games against Charlton Athletic and Blackburn Rovers as four out of six points were collected domestically between the two Champions League encounters against Deportivo de La Coruña.

The visit of Charlton marked the first return to Anfield of Danny Murphy, the two teams being handed the 5.30pm Saturday kick-off, and during the first half there were heavy shades of the Deportivo game as Liverpool controlled proceedings yet frustratingly came unstuck in front of goal, going in for the interval with the scoreline still goalless.

Overcoming an anxious atmosphere almost as much as they did their largely ineffectual opponents, fine second-half goals from John Arne Riise and Luis García clinched Liverpool the three points with eventual ease, a win that kept up their 100 per cent home record in the Premier League and lifted them to fifth in the table on an evening when each answer to a lingering question mark seemed to be replaced by a new quandary.

A clean sheet successfully kept by Chris Kirkland, behind a defence that still looked susceptible to potential errors, García was mixing technical excellence with a physical frailty that saw him drift in and out of the game, while the strike partnership between Milan Baroš and Djibril Cissé once again jarred, with the former's head-down propensity at times leading him down blind alleys out wide, while the latter's continuing profligacy as the club's record signing was attracting escalating scrutiny.

Conversely, this ended up being a commanding victory against opponents who had completed a league double over Liverpool the previous season, led by a manager in Alan Curbishley who had been touted as a possible successor to Gérard Houllier before Anfield attentions turned to Rafael Benítez.

On another day Liverpool could have scored four or five, and every step forward, to the side, and backwards came with a flurry of caveats, meaning that there was no shortage of juxtapositions to mull over. Every positive aspect appeared to have its pocket picked by a negativity that was hiding just around the next corner. The three points obtained against Charlton were warmly welcomed, however, despite the terms and conditions attached.

Three days later, Liverpool were up against more south-east London opposition, this time in the third round of the League Cup and this time away from home, at Millwall. It was to be a sedate night on the pitch but a combustible one in the stands as while Benítez's men overcame the type of understandable early disjointed play that often comes from a team that has made ten changes to their starting line-up, Liverpool eventually cruised to a 3-0 victory to ease their way into the next stage.

It was instead off the pitch where matters became infinitely more heated, the victory coming on an evening that was marred by violent intent after provocation from the home sections resulted in a volatile response in the away end, with seats ripped out and confrontations with police erupting, when after Liverpool had obtained their second goal, an audible section of Millwall's supporters turned their attentions to tragedy chanting, and in some cases, the shocking visual mocking of the recent horrifying killing of Liverpool-born British civil engineer Kenneth Bigley by Islamic extremists in Iraq, on a night when racism had been thick in the air, this on a day when news had broken of the death of the Liverpool-loving radio legend John Peel.

In the days ahead, Millwall would be charged on two fronts: their failure to stop their supporters from making racist chants, and their failure to halt fans from throwing missiles on to the pitch. Liverpool's singular charge related to a failure to prevent their fans from conducting themselves in a threatening, violent or provocative manner.

With Liverpool's supporters kept locked in the away end for almost an hour after the end of the game, by the time they were allowed to exit the stadium the streets of Bermondsey and Southwark were eerily quiet for those of us who were walking back to cars that were parked a mile or so away, while those who had travelled to the game in coaches were being spirited away at speed by accompanying police escorts. The sight of the M25 on the return journey home was a strangely welcome one.

On the pitch, of the ten changes Benítez made, only Djimi Traoré maintained his place in the team from the win against Charlton as in came Jerzy Dudek, Josemi, Stéphane Henchoz, Zak Whitbread, Igor Bišćan, Salif Diao, Stephen Warnock, Darren Potter, Florent Sinama Pongolle, and Neil Mellor, the manager not exactly bashful over projecting his priorities from the off when it came to the domestic cup competitions for 2004/05.

Liverpool had survived a series of early scares which dropped to the usually sharp Neil Harris, before Diao made the 18th-minute breakthrough, netting with a fine half-volley after the ball had been nodded to him by Whitbread via a Warnock corner, but it wasn't until Baroš added the second goal with 20 minutes remaining that Millwall were neutralised as a threat, the Czech scorer having been required to replace the injured Pongolle shortly after the interval, also going on to grab himself another goal in stoppage time.

While Baroš's contributions from the bench proved vital, Pongolle's exit from the game had been unfortunate given that the pace and direct nature of his running had been causing the Millwall defence no shortage of problems, and within four days of their trip to the New Den Liverpool's problems with their striking options would be multiplied exponentially.

With the Premier League trip to Blackburn up next, swiftly to be followed by the critical Champions League mission to La Coruña, the game at Millwall had marked the first of a trio of successive away fixtures across three different competitions, this at a point in time when the team's form on the road had been far more miss than hit. Heading to Ewood Park to take on a Blackburn outfit that had won only one of their first ten league games of the season, losing six – results that had left them rooted to the bottom of the table – this was a game that represented a golden opportunity for Liverpool to pick up a second Premier League away victory of the season and in the process keep themselves within a single figure points tally of leaders Arsenal.

By full time, not only had Liverpool lost out on that much-needed away win, but they had also lost the services of record signing Cissé to what was initially feared to be at best a season-ending, and at worst a career-ending, double leg break of the tibia and fibula. A victim of fate more than of any malice from the innocuous challenge of Jay McEveley that played a key part in the desperately damaging moment, Cissé's departure from the pitch on a stretcher was a devastating blow for the player, his manager, his team-mates, and the supporters in the Darwen End at Ewood Park alike.

This was now a second successive season where Liverpool bones had been broken at Ewood, as in 2003/04 Baroš and Jamie Carragher suffered leg breaks, that while provoking protracted absences, were relatively simple recoveries when compared to the more complicated nature of Cissé's injury. Any prospect of him kicking a ball on a training pitch in 2004/05 was deemed pie in the sky, let alone the idea of him doing so once again on a matchday pitch.

After the 2-2 draw, in which Liverpool played the better football yet also gave their opponents multiple opportunities to win, Benítez wouldn't be drawn in his post-match comments on the seriousness of Cissé's injury, instead choosing to lament the mistakes his team were continuing to make in defence, in particular as they traversed a turbulent first half that swung from obtaining an early lead thanks to John Arne Riise's seventh-minute opener to trailing at the interval, a turn of events that was surely heavily influenced by the nature of the departure of the stricken Cissé.

It was quite apt that Liverpool's second-half equaliser came from Baroš, a player whose future at the club had been under deliberation in the summer but who now found himself to be Benítez's only recognised senior striker, backed up by just the still inexperienced Pongolle, who was marginally out of his teenage years, with the next man in line now being Neil Mellor, who while almost two years older than Pongolle had even less Premier League experience, and had spent his limited first-team football of the previous season being largely played out of position while on loan at West Ham United, who were languishing in the First Division in 2003/04.

For a supporter base that generation on generation had become all-too accustomed to Liverpool having a rich source of guaranteed goals, be it those scored by

Roger Hunt, Kevin Keegan, Kenny Dalglish, David Johnson, Ian Rush, John Aldridge, Robbie Fowler, or Michael Owen, the sudden lack of a truly metronomic striker was something of a culture shock and one which was stoked all the more by the sight of Owen scoring in five successive games for Real Madrid across the fortnight surrounding Cissé's injury: in the Champions League against Dynamo Kyiv, in the league against Valencia, Getafe, and Málaga, and in the Copa del Rey against Leganés.

As November began, it felt as if Real Madrid were goading Liverpool on two fronts, as not only was Owen getting games and scoring goals after his cut price transfer to the Spanish capital but the man who was a hoped-for makeweight in the deal only for José Antonio Camacho to have insisted that he remain at the Santiago Bernabéu, Fernando Morientes, was left frustrated on the sidelines, having slipped to fourth choice behind Owen, Raúl, and Ronaldo.

With the loss of Cissé, the failure to procure Morientes in August stung Liverpool all the more, and despite Camacho having agitated for the player to remain with Real Madrid his own managerial reign at the Santiago Bernabéu was over before the dawning of October, unseated as he was by Florentino Pérez, after a numbing opening-night Champions League defeat at the hands of Bayer Leverkusen, which was followed by a league loss away to Espanyol.

While Cissé's start to life at Anfield had been something of a mixed bag, scoring only twice since his debut goal at White Hart Lane and struggling to form a cohesive working understanding with Baroš, there was nobody else within Benítez's squad who could replicate his brand of power and pace, nor match the potential of where his talents could take him. Yet the spectre of being viewed as Gérard Houllier's signing rather than Benítez's had meant that Cissé had needed to prove himself far more than any other new arrival at Anfield in the summer of 2004, and his injury was a major setback for player and manager.

It all meant that the attacking conundrum for Liverpool, at least until the opening of the winter transfer window, was going to be a tough one to deal with for the next two months, just at a time when their Champions League hopes were resting on a knife edge, sat behind Monaco and Olympiacos with three group games remaining, two of them to be played away, while their record signing's left leg was in plaster, their inspirational captain was still unavailable, and now Alonso was carrying a calf strain.

Heading to Galicia, Liverpool's opponents were still water-treading in mid-table in the league themselves, yet after a poor start to the season Deportivo had gradually become harder to beat since picking off a shock victory away at Real Madrid which kick-started a six-game unbeaten run, inclusive of the goalless draw at Anfield.

During Benítez's first footballing trip back to Spain since becoming Liverpool manager, he returned to his homeland to a welcome of great reverence, with a sense of awe and pride in the air that one of their own had landed one of the most prestigious jobs in the game. Prior to facing Deportivo again, *Marca* had anointed Liverpool as 'The Benitles', enamoured as it was with the concept of a son of Spain being appointed manager of such a grand institution of English and European football, and for whom he had signed a cluster of Spanish players.

Within this bubble of appreciation, Benítez stated that he would be asking his chairman and chief executive to find the funds for some January shopping, primarily to be able to bring in cover for the unfortunate and untimely loss of Cissé. To balance Benítez's January transfer hopes, Liverpool were still struggling to attract investment for the little control that David Moores was willing to cede, and with an announcement in a drop of profits expected in the weeks ahead, it was the worst time imaginable for them to lose their record signing to a broken leg.

It still didn't stop the name game kicking into gear, however, with Morientes being mentioned again, while David Villa, then of Real Zaragoza, was also floated; in the summer of 2005 he would make the move to Benítez's former employers Valencia for €12m. Passing on Villa was to be one of the biggest mistakes of the Benítez era at Anfield.

Ahead of the game, Alonso was running out of time to prove his fitness, and his omission from the starting line-up was a case of Benítez erring on the side of caution. It meant that Dietmar Hamann was to be partnered in central midfield by Igor Bišćan, while without Cissé it meant roles for García and Harry Kewell.

At the Riazor, a once clam-like stadium that looked out to the Atlantic Ocean until the ends behind the goals were filled in, Liverpool procured their first win on Spanish soil for 20 years – since a 1983/84 European Cup victory in Bilbao against Athletic Club – thanks to Jorge Andrade's own goal in the 14th minute.

Liverpool controlled the game and Bišćan was magnificent, setting in motion the move that led to the only goal, bringing the ball out of defence, feeding Riise on the left, who crossed for Baroš to spook Andrade into putting the ball past his own goalkeeper, the once again inspired José Molina. Baroš could have opened the scoring within the first 30 seconds only to be denied by Molina after being sent clear by García, while Riise should have scored just before half-time when laid in by the otherwise anonymous Kewell. Molina was again equal to the challenge, with Riise's follow-up effort being cleared off the goal line, ironically by Andrade.

At the back, Carragher and Sami Hyypiä were in defiant mood, and four group games in they had conceded only one goal, while Bišćan was a revelation in the central playmaker role; with Hamann supplying the protection, the marginalised Croat put in a classic all-round performance, with great composure to go alongside the surprising streak of creativity while also weighing into challenges with a well-timed tenacity.

Covering acres of ground from box to box, Bišćan was effective in breaking up Deportivo forward forays and starting Liverpool moves, casting a spotlight on talents he had rarely been able to display during his time at Anfield. Winning the game by virtue of an own goal might have been unorthodox, but the three points were entirely deserved.

In *The Times*, Benítez said, 'For me, it was the best Liverpool performance I've managed. The important thing for me is not that we won in Spain, because winning in Spain means you have to beat friends, but simply that we won because we had some problems with injuries before the game. The three points mean that our destiny is now in our own hands.'

Olympiacos, 1-0 winners at home to Monaco, were now top of Group A ahead of Liverpool only on the head-to-head rule, both sides now one point ahead of Monaco, while Deportivo sat at the bottom with just two points and were one more adverse result from elimination. For Benítez and his players, they were a win away to Monaco from qualifying for the knockout stage with a game to spare.

Chapter Eight

Ruining Everything

AS LIVERPOOL'S trip to Monaco drew close, there was promising news to be gleaned from the poor domestic form of Didier Deschamps's side, who were beaten at home by Sochaux on the Friday night prior to the visit of Rafael Benítez and his men to the Stade Louis II. This latest loss for the previous season's Champions League runners-up made for their eighth successive Ligue 1 game without a victory. It was now two months since Monaco had won in the league, although they had drawn six of these eight winless fixtures.

Given the turnover of players that Monaco had experienced in the summer of 2004 a degree of turbulence would have been entirely understandable, yet nobody could have expected just how dramatic their fall-off was going to be.

For Deschamps, the task of finding suitable replacements for the likes of Ludovic Giuly and Jérôme Rothen had led him to square pegs for round holes, as neither Javier Saviola nor Ernesto Chevantón could be classed as like-for-like alternatives no matter how talented they were.

As more naturally wide-operating players, Giuly and Rothen had brought greater balance to the line-up, with Saviola and Chevantón both being centrally driven players who had been asked to drift into wide positions whenever possible. The additional losses of Fernando Morientes and Dado Pršo had also meant that there was less attacking variation, although Mohamed Kallon had brought a fresh dimension.

Unlike their form between the two Deportivo de La Coruña games, Liverpool's domestic fortunes since their trip to Galicia had been mixed; the two Premier League defeats that had been suffered at the hands of Birmingham City and Middlesbrough had been very stark setbacks, the former ending a six-game unbeaten run across all competitions and a reversal that constituted Benítez's first loss at Anfield.

Going into the Birmingham game, Liverpool had hauled themselves up to sixth in the Premier League, and with their Champions League group fate now in their own hands they had every reason to feel upbeat and optimistic as Steve Bruce brought his troubled team to Anfield. Without a win on their travels for 11 months, languishing in 16th and having won only one of their opening 11 league fixtures, Birmingham should have posed no problem for a Liverpool side that was beginning to find its feet and was suddenly within reaching distance of the top four. Aside from that, the club from St Andrew's hadn't won at Anfield since 1978.

Injury magnet Darren Anderton climbed from the bench to score the only goal of the game for the visitors, however, with 13 minutes remaining. It was a shock to the system and a reminder that Benítez had much work to do if he was to ensure that Liverpool would return to the Champions League for the following season.

When Anderton plundered Birmingham's clinching goal, it was the first time that they had located the back of the net for 380 minutes; Liverpool had been overcome by a sucker punch, having squandered a string of their own opportunities to score, with Luis García and Dietmar Hamann being guilty of the most culpable misses.

A week on from Djibril Cissé's terrible leg break at Ewood Park, and with Milan Baroš missing due to a strained hamstring, it was on to Florent Sinama Pongolle's shoulders that the burden of procuring goals fell, with Harry Kewell pushed forward in support of him, an experimental strike partnership that lasted for 65 minutes until Pongolle's withdrawal; Steve Finnan was introduced on the right of midfield and García was pushed up front.

Not only were Liverpool labouring in the final third, but this was also an afternoon when Xabi Alonso was introduced to the aesthetic stylings of Robbie Savage in a central midfield meeting of very different minds, while Josemi was given another rough ride at right-back when going up against the subtle yet often penetrating Julian Gray. To add insult to injury, the jettisoned Emile Heskey was a member of the winning Birmingham side, with his first return to Anfield since his summer departure being met by a warm reception from the home support.

Respect being mutual, rather than revelling in a returning victory, Heskey was compassionate in his post-match interviews, particularly towards the struggling Kewell, a player who had now gone 29 games since his last goal in a Liverpool shirt. When Heskey spoke within earshot of Sam Wallace of the *Daily Telegraph*, the former Liverpool striker was candid about the weight of expectation of being responsible for leading the attack at Anfield, stating that you have to concentrate on what you know you can do well and sympathising that Kewell was a winger, not a striker.

Defeat through profligacy, the myopia of Uriah Rennie in not awarding a blatant penalty, the inspired goalkeeping of Maik Taylor, and perhaps overthinking on the part of Benítez, it had seemed an oddity that after such a commanding performance by him against Deportivo, Igor Bišćan wasn't handed the opportunity of building his confidence further, instead left sat on the bench until five minutes from time. There had been carelessness at play in a multitude of respects as Liverpool lost to the type of goal they simply had had no intention of conceding in Galicia.

Four days later, it was a heavily altered line-up that overcame holders Middlesbrough in the fourth round of the League Cup, Neil Mellor scoring both goals in a 2-0 victory in which Zak Whitbread and Darren Potter once again started, and Richie Partridge and John Welsh made cameo appearances from the bench. Much had been hoped of Welsh as a combative midfielder, while Partridge had been a skilful winger, something of a throwback, with a style of a bygone age. The latter hadn't appeared on a Liverpool team sheet for almost three years but he put in a productive 21 minutes, during which he laid on the first of Mellor's two goals, the striker handed a full 90 minutes after having been thrown on as a substitute for the final 18 minutes against Birmingham.

Into the quarter-finals where they were drawn away to Tottenham Hotspur, and the 2004/05 League Cup was fast becoming a platform for Liverpool's youngsters, periphery players, and misfits to make an impression on Benítez. Deposed goalkeeper Jerzy Dudek had been handed the captain's armband at the New Den, and this was again the case at Anfield against Middlesbrough, while the marginalised Stéphane Henchoz was given another game, offering experience in central defence alongside Whitbread. Added to this, Salif Diao – having played quite well at Millwall, even finding the scoresheet – was once again on duty, partnering Bišćan, while Stephen Warnock was recalled too.

Middlesbrough also made wholesale changes to their line-up but boasted the stronger-looking team, inclusive of the future Liverpool players Boudewijn Zenden and Stewart Downing, in a match that for 83 minutes had limped along until Mellor struck twice to spare everyone extra time and the potential of a penalty shoot-out, on a subdued evening when Anfield had paid its respects before kick-off to Emlyn Hughes, who had sadly succumbed to the effects of a brain tumour a day earlier.

In a busy week on home soil, a third game at Anfield within the space of eight days saw Liverpool get back to Premier League winning ways against Crystal Palace, although not without being made to wait until injury time for the decisive goal as the returning Baroš plundered himself a hat-trick, two of his goals from the penalty spot, as they narrowly beat Iain Dowie's stubborn team. Like Birmingham, Palace had been a previously struggling entity that had turned into a team possessed at Anfield.

Back up to sixth and again within touching distance of the top four, Liverpool had leapfrogged their next opponents, Middlesbrough. A seven-day gap until their trip to the Riverside was the perfect opportunity to fine-tune the players' fitness and tactical understanding on the training pitches of Melwood. It also permitted Benítez the time to consider if the returning Steven Gerrard was ready for inclusion or not.

A big plus was that Kewell had come through the entire 90 minutes against Palace, the rewards for a contentious decision by Benítez to disconnect the former Leeds United man from the rest of the first-team squad as part of a personal fitness programme which was designed to bring him into line with the rest of the front-line players.

Kewell's talent was not in doubt, but his fitness and desire were a source of constant conjecture and judgement, at least from supporters and pundits alike. Signed in the summer of 2003 by Gérard Houllier, Liverpool had played on Kewell's boyhood love of the club to see off the challenges of Barcelona, Milan, Arsenal, Chelsea, and Manchester United, to sign a player who had been one of the most exciting individuals in the Premier League while at Elland Road.

At Anfield, Kewell had had a consistent rather than spectacular first season, Houllier's last in charge, but since the arrival of Benítez he had struggled to string a run of consecutive games together. It was a source of huge frustration for the manager, the supporters, and the player himself, but against Palace he had laid on Baroš's second goal and also played the through ball from which the 2004 European Championship Golden Boot winner was brought down, to precipitate the late winner from 12 yards. Nor had these been the only opportunities created by the number seven, and the game represented Kewell's best performance of the season so far, by a considerable margin.

While many of Benítez's players headed off for a ludicrously crowbarred-in midweek international programme of World Cup qualifiers and friendlies, the sight of Gerrard being back in action in all red at Telford, against Wolverhampton Wanderers reserves, was very welcome ahead of the trip to Teesside for a second meeting with Middlesbrough in just ten days. Yet, as Gerrard represented one significant figure returning to action, it was some much-needed relief that was balanced by the trauma of the loss of Baroš, whose involvement in the Czech Republic's encounter with Macedonia in Skopje lasted for just 16 minutes before he suffered a recurrence of his niggling hamstring injury, only this time to more damaging effect, as he would go on to miss Liverpool's next five games, inclusive of the Champions League trip to Monaco.

Heading to Teesside, Liverpool were sat four positions behind fourth-placed Middlesbrough, Steve McLaren's side having lost at home only to José Mourinho's Chelsea, and given the Reds' away record thus far, combined with their lack of a specialist striker, it was perhaps no surprise that they slipped to a 2-0 defeat in a game where the home side were largely in control of proceedings.

Second-best Liverpool might well have been for most of the afternoon, but that still isn't to say that events might have panned out differently given that for the second occasion of the season García had had a perfectly legitimate goal disallowed for offside, while Kewell was also denied by the smart reactions of Mark Schwarzer on a day when the Spaniard and Australian were paired together up front.

Kewell again completed the 90 minutes and Gerrard marked his return to action with 33 minutes as a substitute, replacing Hamann. These were, however, to be the only positives on a forgettable afternoon at the Riverside, during which Chris Riggott scored from close range for his first goal in almost two years, Zenden netted the second, and Downing caused Josemi no shortage of problems.

With little time to lick their wounds, it was to Monte Carlo that Liverpool headed a couple of days later for a game in which victory would have been enough to secure a desperately needed place in the knockout stage of the Champions League with one game to spare, and the cash guarantees that it would bring ahead of some vital shopping in the January transfer window.

Going into this match, if Liverpool's domestic form could be described as inconsistent, Monaco's was abject, with only 2,000 unimpressed spectators having been in attendance for that loss at home to Sochaux, while in the Champions League, since they were beaten at Anfield on the opening night of Group A, Didier Deschamps's team had, however, picked off home victories against Deportivo and Olympiacos, but like Benítez's side, they had lost in Athens to the only goal.

At the Stade Louis II, Monaco had won nine and drawn one of their last ten home Champions League fixtures, and the demand for tickets for the arrival of Liverpool comfortably outran the 15,000 seats that were available. The Monte Carlo public were nothing but selective about what football they were willing to watch.

No Cissé, no Baroš; it was to Mellor that Benítez looked to lead the attack, with García preferred to Kewell to play the link role and Gerrard returning to the starting line-up. Bišćan joined him in midfield with Hamann adding extra steel too, meaning that Alonso was surprisingly stood down to a place among the substitutes, while Finnan got the nod ahead of Josemi at right-back after the latter's recent struggles.

Within just three minutes, the footballing fates had conspired against Liverpool yet again, García's evening swiftly ended by a hamstring injury that would keep him out of action for almost four weeks, inclusive of him missing the crucial final group game against Olympiacos. However, rather than turn to Kewell in terms of a straight swap, Benítez opted to bring on Josemi, pushing Finnan up to the right of midfield with Gerrard slotting in behind Mellor.

Rearrange the seats as he might, nothing would go right for Benítez, all gambles failing to pay off as Liverpool meandered to a 1-0 defeat which, when added to another home win for Olympiacos, meant that they dropped to third place in Group A just as the finish line was coming into view.

In a bruising night on many fronts, Josemi himself had to be withdrawn midway through the second half after a clash of heads with Patrice Evra, an injury that would require 20 stitches, and to add insult to the ever-growing injury list Monaco's winning goal was helped past Chris Kirkland by Saviola, via the use of the Argentine's hand during the build-up.

Six minutes prior to Josemi's exit, Kewell had replaced Djimi Traoré, who had picked up a knee injury, and the exits of both full-backs meant that Finnan and John Arne Riise dropped back to cover in defence, which also brought Stephen Warnock into play, yet no matter what alterations were made by Benítez Liverpool could find no discernible rhythm, while Monaco were only marginally more cohesive themselves in what was a poor game that should have ended in a goalless draw.

Further muddying the waters for Liverpool, Hamann picked up a yellow card which meant he would be suspended for the visit of Olympiacos. Matters could hardly be worse at the end of an evening when a victory would have seen them secure their place in the knockout stage. Now Liverpool had it all to do in order to qualify for the last 16.

Chapter Nine

What a Hit Son

BATTERED AND bruised, as Liverpool limped away from the Stade Louis II following the defeat to Monaco, Rafael Benítez had five days to prepare for the visit to Anfield of Arsenal for a fixture that should have provided an intense sense of foreboding yet instead offered an intriguing challenge of the footballing ethos of the still relatively new manager, and the potential of the vision he was trying to piece together, when going up against Arsène Wenger's stuttering defending champions.

Unbeaten in the Premier League throughout their 2003/04 title-winning campaign, the Invincibles were dripping with talent and trophy-winning intent but had stalled somewhat since their incredible 49-game undefeated run in the league had finally come to an end with an explosive loss at Manchester United five weeks prior to their trip to Anfield.

Wenger's side had made a near-perfect start to the defence of their Premier League championship, winning eight and drawing one of their opening nine games, but since that reversal at Old Trafford they had endured a run of eight games across Premier League and Champions

League with only one victory, contriving to draw six times, and they arrived on Merseyside a little less sure-footed than they had been a month earlier.

This was still a game that on paper Liverpool had no right to win, as from the bench alone Wenger could call upon Robin van Persie, while out on the pitch he had at his disposal a peak Thierry Henry, supplemented in attack by the gifts of Robert Pires and the ultimately tragic José Antonio Reyes, supported by a midfield of Patrick Vieira, Freddie Ljungberg, and Cesc Fàbregas, backed by a defence that was marshalled by Sol Campbell, Kolo Touré, Ashley Cole, and Lauren, an outrageously talented team that had the goalkeeping of Jens Lehmann to fall back upon.

In contrast, Liverpool were missing seven of their first-team squad, and Neil Mellor was again to lead the attack, this time alongside Florent Sinama Pongolle, while their best attacking alternative from the bench was the belatedly available Antonio Núñez whose only combative preparation since his return from injury had been a run-out against Leeds United's reserves.

Across the rest of Benítez's line-up, the losses of Josemi and Djimi Traoré forced the manager to deploy Steve Finnan and John Arne Riise in the full-back positions, meaning that naming a conservative midfield was off the menu. Dietmar Hamann played the defensive midfield role, Xabi Alonso was the playmaker, Steven Gerrard was nominally on the right but with the remit to rove, and Harry Kewell was deployed on the left. An inexperienced partnership up front aside, it made for a perfectly balanced team and one with the potential to hit and hit hard.

Liverpool were wonderful against Arsenal in a game that served as a window upon what Benítez could create at Anfield, given the funds and better fortune to do so. The players in all red were by far the best team for almost an hour, and when Vieira clipped the ball over the advancing Chris Kirkland as the goalkeeper went to ground in the 57th minute to procure the visitors the equaliser, it was entirely against the run of play.

Alonso had opened the scoring from the edge of the Arsenal penalty area four minutes before the interval, latching on to a beautifully weighed ball from Gerrard played with the outside of the right foot, in turn having been served by a magnificent cushioned header from Kewell after a tremendous diagonal pass by Finnan.

On an afternoon when Anfield was bouncing, Liverpool were magnificent, and they should have had an early penalty when Gerrard was caught by Touré's trailing leg. In a game that set out at a breakneck speed, the officials were again struggling to keep up with the pace of play when Mellor was set free inside the Arsenal penalty area by Riise, from where the crossbar was struck, only for the linesman's flag to be erroneously raised.

Rather than kill the mood music, Liverpool kept up the pressure and when the opening goal came it was fully deserved. With the Reds continuing to dominate play as the second half began, when Arsenal's equaliser came it was out of nowhere, yet it was also a fittingly stylish contribution to the game as Vieira linked wonderfully with Henry and Pires, to navigate a way through a determined home defence. In a more even game after the equaliser, both teams had their turn at dictating the pace, but chances were kept to a minimum until Mellor stepped up two minutes into injury time.

With a draw looking increasingly likely, Hamann earned a free kick from Henry close to Kirkland's right-hand corner flag, just as Arsenal were attempting to force a late goal of their own; the goalkeeper sent a long, percentage-playing ball that landed centrally, around 40 yards to the Kop goalmouth, kicking on as it did toward Kewell, who got into a tangle for possession with Campbell and Touré. The Liverpool number seven went to ground arguably in the hope of winning another free kick, this time within shooting distance.

The ball seemed to bounce off the side of Kewell's face and then the back of Campbell's head as the latter clattered the former, diverting it straight into the path of the on-running Mellor, who despite being closed in on at speed by Vieira got his shot in first. Catching it beautifully with his right foot, the ball swept past the outstretched hand of Jens Lehmann before it bounced off the turf and into the net.

Bedlam erupted in front of the Kop, and on all four sides of Anfield it was an ocean of delirious humanity, apart from the enclave to the left-hand side of the lower Anfield Road section. This was a win of huge purpose, and it was the perfect riposte to those Arsenal supporters who had mocked the Gérard Houllier Liverpool vintage as hoofers of the ball, mainly in their lingering angst at the outcome of the 2001 FA Cup Final.

On the Kop that day, a new song to the tune of 'La Bamba', in honour of Benítez and the Spanish players he had brought along to the club, began as a bit of a murmur, and three days later at White Hart Lane in the League Cup quarter-final it really took flight on what was one of the best domestic occasions of Liverpool's 2004/05 campaign.

Again making clear where his priorities rested, despite many Liverpool supporters feeling that Benítez should go strong with his line-up to face Tottenham Hotspur, it was once more a collection of outcasts and kids who took to the field in north London despite the prospect of another trip to Cardiff's Millennium Stadium starting to draw within sight.

Of the 11 players fielded by Benítez against Tottenham, nine of them had started earlier ties against Millwall and Middlesbrough, denoting the pattern of a defined subsection of his squad that was earmarked for this competition, and he wasn't for changing direction yet despite home manager Martin Jol pulling absolutely no punches in his choice of line-up, choosing internationals of the calibre of Paul Robinson, Ledley King, Anthony Gardner, Reto Ziegler, Timothée Atouba, Michael Carrick, Frédéric Kanouté, and Robbie Keane, while another two would be thrown into the fray from the bench in the shapes of Jermain Defoe and Pedro Mendes.

For Liverpool, Jerzy Dudek returned in goal, handed the captain's armband once more, with Stéphane Henchoz

WHAT A HIT SON

and Zak Whitbread again the central defensive pairing. Stephen Warnock was called on once more, this time asked to cover left-back in the absence of Djimi Traoré, while David Raven was handed a debut at right-back.

In midfield, Igor Bišćan was yet again joined by Salif Diao and Darren Potter, where they were now complimented by Antonio Núñez, who was making his first senior start for Liverpool after having been given 20 minutes or so from the bench against Arsenal. Up front, Mellor and Pongolle were the only players to translate from the team that had beaten Wenger's side three days earlier.

Not even opting for an element of experience on the bench as he had done against Millwall and Middlesbrough, apart from Kirkland being the back-up goalkeeper, Benítez went all in on inexperience with Richie Partridge the senior member, ahead of John Welsh, who was only just out of his teens, plus Mark Smyth and Robbie Foy who weren't yet in their 20s.

On face value, it appeared that the tie was being viewed as collateral damage by Benítez in his pursuit of a place in the knockout stage of the Champions League and a top-four spot in the Premier League. Fresh out of a six-game losing streak during which Jacques Santini had resigned as manager after only a short few months in the job, for Tottenham it very much looked as if Jol was wanting to grasp the opportunity of a domestic cup semi-final berth with both hands, this after his team had defeated Middlesbrough just a couple of hours prior to Liverpool turning Arsenal over.

With one eye clearly fixed upon an opportunistic domestic cup bounce within the early weeks of his reign, the fact that Jol could almost reach out and touch a potential trip to Cardiff was an almost incredulous concept, and as he handed in a team sheet that included four England internationals in the starting 11 plus two more on the bench – with the added advantage of home soil – it suggested anything other than a Tottenham victory would have been an act of defiance mixed in with a dash of the absurd.

By rights it should have been a simple evening for the home team, but backed by a phenomenal away section Liverpool pulled off the ridiculous. As the game lurched into extra time and onward to a penalty shoot-out, Benítez's collection of kids and misfits put in superhuman shifts, with those on the pitch inspiring those of us in the not so cheap seats, and vice-versa. It was the first day of December and it was as if Liverpool's supporters had decided upon throwing an early Christmas party at White Hart Lane regardless of the outcome of the result.

Thrown a succession of curve balls, Benítez lost the services of Mellor early in the second half, which brought Welsh into play, isolating Pongolle as a lone striker. Added to this, Núñez understandably ran out of steam with 20 minutes remaining of the initial 90, but instead of turning to Partridge Benítez threw on Smyth, a winger with an impressive turn of pace.

For much of the evening the flow of the game meandered in the expected direction, and it was a combination of the belligerent goalkeeping of Dudek and the profligacy of the home team that guided proceedings into extra time, but when Defoe finally broke the Liverpool resistance in the 107th minute – slotting home a low centre from Kanouté – nobody would have been surprised had Tottenham gone on to take full advantage of the tiring legs of their visitors and claimed themselves another goal or two,

Yet, after being part of the solution for Jol with his role in Defoe's goal, Kanouté then made himself complicit in the problem when handling the ball in his own penalty area four minutes from the end to gift Liverpool a penalty that Pongolle gleefully converted to take the tie to a shoot-out from 12 yards.

Having been reduced to a show of character from the penalty spot, the pressure was entirely the preserve of the home team with Michael Brown scooping his effort over Dudek's crossbar, this after the Pole had already saved from Kanouté, events that rendered Potter's miss with the visitors' third spot-kick redundant as Henchoz, Partridge, Welsh, and finally Pongolle each put the ball past Robinson to spark wild celebrations in the away section and on the pitch.

In a show of utter defiance, Liverpool had progressed to the semi-finals of the League Cup completely against the odds, while Tottenham were left to count the cost of their own carelessness, and in particular Kanouté's part in proceedings, on an evening when he had struck the crossbar, seen some fine opportunities he had provided for team-mates squandered, laid on the opening goal, given away the penalty that levelled the game, and then missed from the spot in the shoot-out.

Yet it wasn't all about basic belligerence and riding their luck for this pic'n'mix of a Liverpool team, as they could have had the game won themselves within the 90 minutes; Pongolle was a constant danger to the Tottenham defence, Gardner being lucky to avoid a red card when dragging the striker back after he broke free and clean through on goal deep into the second half.

There was no shortage of heroes of the Liverpool cause at White Hart Lane, with Dudek making a string of fine saves, Raven excellent at right-back, making one astonishing tackle on Defoe during extra time, and Welsh covering every blade of grass on multiple occasions. It was a victory born of the hardest of work, and it was the perfect feelgood follow-up to the win over Arsenal.

Positive vibes on the pitch, but it was very different mood music the following night at a stormy annual general meeting as club chairman David Moores and chief executive Rick Parry had to fend off hostility over their ongoing search for fresh investment, with the wife of the Redrow building supremo Steve Morgan particularly vocal on the subject of her husband's attempts to push through a deal worth a prospective £70m to Liverpool.

It was with animosity in the air that Moores and Parry publicly announced record club losses of £21.9m, and a £35m escalation on original projections of the cost of the proposed new stadium that was earmarked to be constructed on Stanley Park, which were added to the existing £13m overdraft that was divulged 12 months earlier. It made for a volatile evening where while Moores and Parry were disclosing significant debts, the Morgans were playing the role of the repelled answer to the problem, with Terry Smith, one of the other directors, feeling compelled to bring up weighty questions about the structure of the offer that was on the table. With the temperature rising, Moores stated that he would consider stepping down should a suitable investor be found, citing the levels of stress that he was suffering.

Disagreements aplenty and sides being chosen, whether it was in accepting Morgan's money or not, the rank-and-file shareholders in attendance clearly wanted some form of renewal at boardroom level, and on a show of hands there was clear opposition to the re-election to the directorship of Noel White and Les Wheatley, who had retained their positions by proxy ballot already, rendering the shareholder vote nothing more than a noted protest.

However, at least on one point, those in attendance at the AGM were in agreement as an emphatic show of hands confirmed that there was no appetite in the room to yield their exclusivity arrangement for the planned stadium for Stanley Park, after recent pressure had been put on the club to look into the possibility of entering into a groundshare plan with Everton. Just what Benítez made of it all is open to conjecture, yet he utilised his ten minutes at the microphone to illustrate what he felt was a sense of unity at the club, the likes of which he had never experienced at Valencia.

As Benítez shifted his attentions back to matters on the pitch, and aiming to consolidate the precarious nature of the strength of his squad, he was now open to the idea of extending Hamann's stay at the club, the German international having proved himself a more consistent option in the defensive midfield role than either Bišćan or Diao, although in terms of potential January recruits the manager was now being linked with Iván Campo in a potential exchange deal to make El Hadji Diouf's loan spell at Bolton Wanderers a permanent transfer.

Liverpool's last game before the crunch visit of Olympiacos took them to the Midlands to face David O'Leary's Aston Villa, who were sat one position and one point ahead of Benítez's side going into the encounter and had so far experienced a campaign that at least domestically was a mirror image of Liverpool's.

Impressive and unbeaten at home, Villa's problems had been on their travels, winning only one of their first eight league games on the road, but at Villa Park they had kept five clean sheets from seven, so like Liverpool there was a Jekyll and Hyde nature at play for O'Leary's side, although the bare stats of Villa's home record and Liverpool's away from Anfield pointed towards another tough assignment for Benítez and his team.

Under Gérard Houllier, however, Liverpool had enjoyed a fine record at Villa Park, and hadn't lost there since the days of Roy Evans, a run stretching to seven with their last reversal away to Villa being over six and a half years since. In terms of muscle memory for Liverpool's longer-serving players and their travelling supporters, Villa Park felt like a safe haven, a venue where they had also won an FA Cup semi-final under Houllier in April 2001.

For 44 minutes Liverpool's first-half performance suggested another productive day would be enjoyed at the expense of Villa: Gerrard a blur of running and shooting power, Alonso displaying a masterclass in passing, and Kewell on a mission to silence the pre-match musings of his former Leeds United manager O'Leary, who prior to the game seemed keener to talk up the Australian's struggles for form rather than the capabilities of his own team.

Kewell opened the scoring in the 16th minute, his first goal for Liverpool since February, and try as he and his team-mates might, what would have been a deserved second goal didn't materialise, and they found themselves undone just before the interval through an excellent free kick by Nolberto Solano after Carragher had been hard done by in the awarding of the set piece.

With a cluster of chances for Gerrard and an opportunity for Mellor to make a hero of himself again, Liverpool should have taken all three points, and O'Leary was magnanimous enough afterwards to admit that Villa had been fortunate to avoid defeat. Despite the two points dropped and the understandable frustrations, there were plenty of positives for Benítez to return to Merseyside with, and in particular the performance of Kewell, who worked tirelessly for the full 90 minutes, the last half an hour of which were spent as the lone striker after the withdrawal of Mellor.

With the narrative from Villa Park having been one of swings and roundabouts for Benítez, the manager and his players had little in the way of time to brood over the fumbling of what would have been only their second away win of the season in the Premier League as their date with Champions League Group A destiny against Olympiacos was up next: a game upon which the outcome would entirely dictate the very future of the club.

When wheeled out for the pre-match press conference 24 hours before the game, Benítez and his captain clearly hadn't aligned the theme of their answers to the questions that would be posed. The manager, while stating that he expected a victory from his team, did not see the alternative of dropping into the UEFA Cup as detrimental, whereas Gerrard billed such a prospect as a disaster.

Gerrard was then further drawn on his future at the club once more, with his reissuing of the basics for the need for swift improvement if he and Liverpool were to win trophies of substance together, candid words that were quite rightly translated by the headline writers as a hint toward an impending exit in the summer, leaving little in the way of column inches for insights on the match at hand.

With a UEFA Cup winners' medal in his pocket from 2001 and another two campaigns in the very same tournament taken part in since, it was understandable that Gerrard felt his time in European club football's second-tier event had run its course. At the season's end, Gerrard would be about to turn 25, and it was only right that he felt he had to be playing on European nights in the Champions League rather than the UEFA Cup.

Bridging that gap for Gerrard, in Liverpool being able to contend for Champions League and Premier League success, was all that mattered and should Benítez be unable to provide clear evidence of a viable route to such glories then the captain would have to seriously consider chasing those medals elsewhere. The message was writ large.

Yet within the subconscious of Gerrard, there had to be massive doubts that his core requirements to stay could be met at all. In *The Times* on the morning of the Olympiacos game, not for the last time during 2004/05, he was quoted over a lack of belief that Liverpool could win the Champions League that season, instead erring on pragmatism when stating, 'I have to be realistic and say we're not going to win the Champions League this season, but I do think we can improve on the quarter-finals, which we achieved a few years ago.'

To be fair, with a big hurdle still to clear just to put Liverpool's name in the Perspex orb for the draw for the knockout stage, at this point a dose of realism was no bad thing. Gerrard would be riding into the midfield battle with Rivaldo to worry about, and no Hamann to back him up thanks to the one-match suspension he was serving after the yellow card he had been flashed away to Monaco.

Another tale of one in, one out, Hamann's absence was at least offset by the return of Baroš, although the Czech striker could have done with a domestic tune-up first-team run out beforehand rather than being airdropped straight back into the starting line-up. In terms of player availability, Benítez still seemed to be welcoming squad members back with the shake of one hand while waving another off to the sidelines with the other.

Olympiacos's form leading up to the game had been excellent. Beaten only once so far in the league, four days prior to arriving at Anfield they had beaten Panathinaikos to go top of the Alpha Ethniki, while they had won all three of their home Champions League games, although conversely had not won on their travels in 23 previous away days in the competition.

It was into a cauldron of noise that Gerrard led his team-mates out of the Anfield tunnel for what would be a night of sheer tension and eventually unbridled delirium. Yet at half-time all hopes of progress appeared to be dashed as Liverpool trailed 1-0 to a marvellous Rivaldo free kick, the Brazilian's Olympiacos colleagues indulging in an impressive display of spoiling tactics and stout defending either side of their goal as they unapologetically aimed to knock Liverpool out of their stride with home frustrations growing.

A 1-0 deficit was scant half-time reward for Liverpool, Benítez's side having been emphatically on the front foot for much of a first half during which they had forced eight corners, seen a Baroš header cleared off the line, another from Sami Hyypiä go into the side-netting, and an Alonso free kick strike the post via the ball being flicked off the back of the heel of Gerrard's right boot.

With the added caveat that Monaco were 3-0 up at the interval away to Deportivo, the head-to-head rule meant that Liverpool now needed to win by two clear goals, and Benítez responded by removing Traoré from the fray, dropping Riise to left-back, switching Kewell wide and bringing on Pongolle in support of Baroš through the middle.

Within two minutes of the restart Kewell had laid on the equaliser for Pongolle and the touch paper had been lit, although it would be an agonising further 32 minutes until this time Pongolle turned provider as his cross caused panic in the Olympiacos penalty area, from where a header by Núñez was only parried by Antonis Nikopolidis to the feet of the opportunistic Mellor, who drove the ball into the Kop end net.

Mellor had only been on the pitch for two minutes as a replacement for the exhausted Baroš, and his goal created bedlam around an electrified stadium, teeing up a final ten minutes where anything seemed possible yet during which a desperately noble exit would have fitted the storyline of the season so far for Liverpool perfectly.

But then came the iconic moment for Gerrard; a move that began with Riise losing possession of the ball due to over-impetuosity only for Carragher to take control of the situation, throwing in an unexpected Cruyff turn before ignoring the pleas from Gerrard of a square ball to instead send in a fine cross which led to Mellor's cushioned header into the path of his captain, the ball dropping temptingly to him just outside the D of the penalty area. With only four minutes remaining, what came next was the ultimate comic book finish in front of Gerrard's adoring public as his shot bulged into the back of the net, before he ran off to the left to be enveloped by his team-mates and supporters alike.

Even the calm and collected Benítez found himself swept up in the moment, embraced in his technical area by a jubilant, orange-jacketed steward, on an evening when the blueprint of what was to come in Istanbul five months later was sketched out.

Throughout the game, Alonso had been magnificent, something that goes largely forgotten within the shadow of Gerrard's scene-stealing heroics, while Kewell and Núñez had worked diligently in helping Liverpool turn the screw on their increasingly bedraggled opponents. Added to this, Baroš's pace had regularly stretched the Olympiacos defence, while Pongolle was the very image of energy, skill, and determination, and the late contribution of a goal and an assist from Mellor was priceless.

Dysfunction and genius had colluded with one another for Benítez, Gerrard and his team-mates, and the springboard it had created was about to send them to the moon. Drama aplenty: Gerrard had seen a goal disallowed, Baroš adjudged to have been too forceful in leading for a challenge for the ball with his arm, and Nikopolidis spilling the shot beneath his body and into the net.

It was a harsh decision and a let-off for Olympiacos at the time, while there had been other chances prior to the introduction of Mellor, one of which Kewell should have done better with when presented with a header from a Pongolle cross, but there was simply no denying Gerrard and Liverpool their moment of sweet glory and a place in the last 16.

Chapter Ten

Big Pharma

MAYBE OVERSTIMULATED within the slipstream of the glorious chaos and drama of their victory over Olympiacos, Liverpool's immediate response to reaching the knockout stages of the 2004/05 Champions League was to take only one point from the next six that were available to them in the Premier League, lurching straight into a Merseyside derby defeat at Goodison Park in a game that kicked off just 63 hours after Rafael Benítez's team had walked from the pitch at Anfield on such an intoxicating high.

David Moyes's Everton had enjoyed a surprisingly impressive first third of their Premier League campaign, this despite being dispossessed of the talents of Wayne Rooney, who had been swallowed up by Manchester United within the wake of his magnificent performances for England at the 2004 European Championship in Portugal.

Going into the derby, Everton were sat third in the table, four places and nine points ahead of Liverpool, but for Benítez the glimmer of light was that with a game in hand, a win at Goodison would be enough to cut the gap to six points with potentially another three in lieu, plus Everton were still to travel to Anfield later in the season. Stepping stones were there for Liverpool to play catch-up, yet it was crucial that they were able to put a positive first foot forward in what was the 200th Merseyside derby. Benítez had got so much right with his decisions against Arsenal and Olympiacos, even within the draw at Aston Villa too, but at Goodison the five changes he made to his starting line-up took the spring out of Liverpool's stride against opponents who had a settled side, one for which Moyes was keeping personnel changes to a minimum.

Milan Baroš, after his exertions against Olympiacos, was rested completely by Benítez, whereas Steve Finnan, Djimi Traoré, Antonio Núñez, and most questionably of all, Xabi Alonso were all stood down to the bench as in came Josemi, Dietmar Hamann, Salif Diao, Florent Sinama Pongolle, and Neil Mellor.

Josemi's return projected Benítez's perseverance of thought that the former Málaga defender might still be a better bet at right-back ahead of Finnan, and while Hamann's reappearance after his suspension for the Olympiacos game made sense, the fielding of Diao instead of Alonso was to limit the fluidity of Liverpool's performance and in turn give Everton's five-man midfield less to worry themselves about. Meanwhile, for their contributions from the bench in midweek, Pongolle and Mellor were deployed up front from the start.

It was a team selection that self-hamstrung Liverpool for the game, and after having spent the first hour or so of proceedings keeping himself up close and personal to Steven Gerrard, Lee Carsley scored the only goal of the afternoon midway through the second half, catching out a partially unsighted Chris Kirkland.

Frustratingly, Liverpool had had their opportunities to take something from a day when Nigel Martyn was in inspired form and Tim Cahill made a desperate goal-line clearance. While Everton had undeniably been the surprise package of the season so far, and their win lifted them into second place behind Chelsea, they hadn't been faultless on home soil, as while they had consistently seen off the rank and file they had lost against higher-calibre opponents, beaten at Goodison by Arsenal and Tottenham Hotspur, and by Chelsea on the road in the league, while Arsène Wenger's side had also unseated them in the League Cup.

This was Liverpool's first derby day defeat since September 1999, and it marked the end of a run of three successive wins at Goodison, Gérard Houllier largely having enjoyed the supremacy in his battles with Moyes and, before him, Walter Smith. For Benítez, however, it had been an inglorious introduction to the fixture, although one with valuable lessons filed for other meetings.

It was a sobering reminder that there was much to do to turn Liverpool into a team that could string an extended run of positive results together, and between the victory over Olympiacos in early December and the first leg of the last-16 tie at home to Bayer Leverkusen towards the tail-end of February, beginning with the loss to Everton Benítez oversaw 15 domestic fixtures –

12 in the Premier League, two in the League Cup, and one in the FA Cup – winning eight, drawing one, and losing six.

A continuing image of inconsistency, in the league Liverpool won at home against Newcastle United, Southampton, and Fulham, and away to West Bromwich Albion, Norwich City, and Charlton Athletic, yet were defeated not only at Goodison but also at St Mary's and St Andrews against Southampton and Birmingham City, the latter completing an unedifying double over Benítez's team, while reversals were also suffered at home to Chelsea and Manchester United. Meanwhile, in the domestic cups, there were wildly differing experiences as while Watford were beaten home and away to earn a place in the League Cup Final, there was only ignominy to be garnered at Turf Moor against Burnley in the FA Cup.

With Anfield in a subdued mood three days beyond the loss to Everton, the midweek visit of Portsmouth did little to lift spirits as a goalless and insipid first half was followed by 45 minutes in which a draw was snatched from the jaws of victory, Gerrard's 70th-minute free kick finding the top corner of Jamie Ashdown's net only to be cancelled out by Lomana LuaLua's gift of a headed equaliser in stoppage time.

Again, Liverpool had been all too generous in their profligacy, with Ashdown making saves of varying degrees of taxation from Harry Kewell, Hamann, and Núñez, and the longer the game stretched without the home side obtaining a second goal the more a sense of foreboding crept into proceedings.

Benítez had made another set of sweeping changes to his line-up with six alterations to the team that had started at Goodison, as back in came not only Finnan, Traoré, Alonso, Núñez, and Baroš, in place of Josemi, Riise, Diao, Pongolle, and Mellor, but also the deposed first-choice goalkeeper Jerzy Dudek, in place of the injured Kirkland, who had not trained since the defeat to Everton after waking on the Sunday morning with a searing back pain that would eventually require new year surgery, thus unwittingly and prematurely ending his season, and ultimately his career at Anfield.

A domino effect having been set in motion, Kirkland would never play a first-team game for Liverpool again, moving on to Wigan Athletic a year and a half later via an initial loan spell at the DW Stadium and also a season-long loan at West Bromwich Albion in 2005/06, where further injuries hampered him at The Hawthorns, before rebuilding his fortunes with Wigan.

Prior his back injury, Kirkland had come under increasing scrutiny for his place in the team with questions being asked about his reactions to the goals conceded against Aston Villa, Olympiacos, and Everton, although Benítez had made a point of publicly backing him; yet Dudek's return against Portsmouth was the big Pole's opportunity to impress, only for his late misjudgement of a Matthew Taylor cross to be the key to LuaLua's equaliser. There and then, the die had arguably been definitively cast that a new goalkeeper would be arriving in the summer.

It was to Anfield that Liverpool's bewildered supporters flocked again five days later for the visit of Graeme Souness's Newcastle, and as an indication of just how their resolve was being tested by the wild fluctuations of Benítez's team the difference in attendances between the midweek encounter with Portsmouth and the arrival of a former Liverpool legend as a player, but one who oversaw a turbulent and controversial era at Anfield as manager, weighed in at just under 9,000 fewer souls.

Given the concerning financial outlook that was divulged at the recent annual general meeting, with just a shade over 35,000 in attendance for the Portsmouth game it will have been a relief to David Moores and Rick Parry that those clicking through the turnstiles five days later ticked upward to close on the 44,000 barrier; those extra supporters were rewarded with three much-needed points and a result that was to be the first of a valuable trio of Premier League victories to close out 2004.

The Newcastle match was one of those that can only be termed as a bit of a chaos, where the mood lighting was set before kick-off when Craig Bellamy contrived to injure himself during the warm-up, and just beyond the half-hour Liverpool's defence was bearing gifts once again when Patrick Kluivert was able to convert from close range.

Thankfully, just six minutes after falling behind, Liverpool found themselves ahead with Titus Bramble being unnerved enough in his own penalty area by the looming presence of Sami Hyypiä to divert the ball past his own goalkeeper, Shay Given, before the returning Mellor grabbed his team the lead prior to the interval.

Still, with all second-half narratives possible, when Baroš added Liverpool's third on the hour even the most nervous of dispositions would have been soothed by the later sight of Lee Bowyer being flashed a red card by Graham Poll after a wild challenge on Pongolle within minutes of the Frenchman's introduction as a substitute in place of Mellor.

Plenty of positives to be taken by Benítez: Alonso was once again outstanding, Kewell was showing flashes of the player of old that Liverpool supporters were demanding him to be, while the manager was also able to welcome back the returning Luis García, who was playing his first competitive football since damaging his hamstring away to Monaco three and a half weeks earlier.

While the split personality of the 2004/05 Liverpool could take nothing for granted, the fixture list now offered them back-to-back Christmas week dates with the two teams that were propping the rest of the Premier League up – firstly away at West Brom and then at home to Southampton, a golden opportunity to close the gap to a place in the top four with Manchester United six points ahead and in possession of the last Champions League berth.

Liverpool ran riot at The Hawthorns, clocking up a 5-0 success, a margin of victory that should have been much wider and one that owed almost as much to the sending-off of Cosmin Contra shortly before the interval than it did the endeavour and enthusiasm of visitors who would have been difficult to deny, even had West Brom been the team with the advantage of the extra man.

Two goals from Riise, and one each for Pongolle, Gerrard, and García, and even the comedic nature of a penalty miss by Baroš couldn't disrupt Liverpool's momentum; less than 48 hours later it was back to Anfield for a more circumspect 1-0 win over Harry Redknapp's Southampton with Pongolle striking for the second successive game.

Given the outcome against Portsmouth a fortnight earlier, an increasing anxiety gripped Anfield during the latter stages of proceedings after a cluster of opportunities for further goals were once again spurned, with Riise rattling Antti Niemi's crossbar, and the Finnish international also tipping a García effort on to the post. Michael Owen, watching on from the directors' box while enjoying the Spanish league's winter break, would surely have grimaced about the lack of a cutting edge, an issue he had helped create by his departure for Real Madrid.

By no means a flawless performance, three more handy points were offset by the early exit of a badly limping Finnan, and Benítez was moved to confirm in his post-match press conference that with the January transfer window soon to be opened, activity by Liverpool was imminent. The groundswell of opinion seemed to point in the direction that the arrival of Fernando Morientes was all but a done deal, while rumours of interest in Nicolas Anelka continued to bob to the surface.

Still six points adrift of the Champions League positions as 2004 came to an end, rather than Manchester

United being the target to chase in fourth, now the focus was Everton after they had slipped to defeat away at Charlton Athletic, and January's fixture list for Liverpool was one that offered a combination of some big Anfield challenges but also cause for optimism.

Whatever light that had appeared at the end of the Premier League tunnel over Christmas was soon to dim, however, as Liverpool went on to lose three of their four league games across the opening month of 2005: beaten narrowly at home by Chelsea and Manchester United and meekly away at Southampton, the reversal at St Mary's coming just three and a half weeks after having defeated the same opponents at Anfield.

Against Chelsea, Liverpool displayed enough endeavour to win the game and they certainly didn't deserve to lose, yet fate smiled fondly upon the visitors instead, while the referee Mike Riley chose a bad day to indulge in poor decisions as twice he denied Benítez's side blatant penalties, one when Tiago handled the ball in full view of the official who had his whistle in his mouth, and the other when Claude Makélélé brought down Pongolle.

A mentally draining and damaging afternoon for Liverpool, the game was bookended by Frank Lampard's breaking of Alonso's ankle and Joe Cole's winning goal, which was deflected off Carragher and beyond the helpless Dudek. After three successive wins, it was a shuddering slap in the face and a significant blow to Liverpool's still fragile confidence.

Shoulders slumped as Liverpool's players took their leave of the pitch, while Chelsea's headed down to the

Anfield Road end to celebrate with the away section, there was at least the passion and anger of Carragher to take solace in as he followed the scurrying Riley down the tunnel for a bout of finger-jabbing fury, and to launch a well-directed tirade of opinion over the lack of quality in his refereeing.

José Mourinho, undoubtedly because he surely didn't view Liverpool as a title-challenging threat, was magnanimous enough to concede afterwards that his team had been lucky to claim the victory and that the Reds had provided the toughest test that his Premier League champions-in-the-making had so far faced; yet for all of the home side's promise and ingenuity on the ball, Chelsea's defence had remained obstinately impenetrable.

With the added ingredients of Alonso's broken ankle and the penalties that never were, the Machiavellian role of the moustache-twirling Victorian-era villain had been enthusiastically grasped by Chelsea, and across the three further fixtures that the two teams would face one another in before the season's end Mourinho himself would take to the theme with increasing relish.

Less than 48 hours beyond the final whistle being blown by Riley at Anfield, Liverpool were back in Premier League action when they were again handed the early kick-off slot, on the January bank holiday Monday, their supporters dealt the punishing and unforgiving road trip to Carrow Road for the clash with Norwich City.

Having played well only to lose against Chelsea, Liverpool flipped that concept in Norfolk by winning on a day when they weren't hitting the high notes, with

García's excellent opening goal shortly before the hour being somewhat at odds with the low quality of the wider game that surrounded it, before Riise took advantage six minutes later of a loose ball in Robert Green's penalty area to make it 2-0.

Cruising to a sedate victory, Liverpool still contrived to make heavy weather of matters late in the game by conceding in the 88th minute to a fine Matt Jarvis finish and surviving injury-time penalty claims with Howard Webb waving protests away after Carragher had tussled with Gary Doherty, this being Norwich's second shout of the second half after an earlier Darren Huckerby cross struck Carragher's hand at close quarters, both claims erring more towards straw-clutching shouts rather than the blatant nature of the spot-kicks that Liverpool were denied against Chelsea.

With Gerrard dynamic in midfield, García an intermittent threat, and Carragher marshalling the backline marvellously, inspiration was harder to glean from the rest of their team-mates, with the recalled Diao putting in a performance that made Alonso's long absence ahead feel all the starker, and Núñez drifting on the periphery in an overtly lightweight manner that didn't bode well for what he might be able to contribute against tougher opposition.

Offsetting the three crucial points won at Norwich, the injury outlook darkened across the following days with surgery confirmed for Kirkland, acceptance sinking in that Alonso would not be back within the initial estimated timescale of six weeks to two months, and

THERE ARE PLACES I REMEMBER

that surgery would be necessary for him too. Increasingly down to the bare bones with his squad, Benítez's need for reinforcements was now reaching critical mass.

Within 48 hours of the victory at Carrow Road, the first of those reinforcements had arrived with the free transfer of Mauricio Pellegrino from Valencia, the veteran Argentine central defender coming in as cover for Carragher and Hyypiä, an arrival that would pave the way for Stéphane Henchoz to depart for Celtic three weeks later, this after discussions with Rangers and Charlton Athletic came to nothing.

One new arrival in, Benítez had begun to play hardball with Real Madrid over the long-speculated signing of Fernando Morientes, issuing a 48-hour deadline for progress to be made and insisting that otherwise he would turn his attentions elsewhere, with Nicolas Anelka's name still being thrown into the mix of sports page headlines.

Muddying the waters when it came to Morientes was that Madrid were now on their third head coach of the season, with José Antonio Camacho and Mariano García Remón both having fallen on their swords before the turn of the year, leading to the nomadic Vanderlei Luxemburgo now being at the helm, events that threw ambiguity on to prospective January transfer business at the Santiago Bernabéu.

While Benítez remained confident that he would eventually get his man, and Morientes had a genuine will to sign for Liverpool if there was to be no future for him with Madrid, it was still proving to be a struggle to get the deal over the finish line. Added to the Morientes chatter, the prospects of Scott Carson being recruited from Leeds United were escalating daily, although Chelsea were also keeping tabs on the soon to be out of contract teenager. Alternatives mooted with regards the now pressing need for goalkeeping cover included Madrid's César Sánchez, and Ali Al-Habsi, Lyn Oslo's Oman international shot-stopper who would eventually go on to play Premier League football for Bolton Wanderers and Wigan Athletic.

In the meantime, in the absence of Kirkland, Dudek's prime understudy was the 20-year-old Paul Harrison, who had come through the Liverpool youth system to sign professional terms in May 2004. Harrison, who as a young child had lost his father and uncle at the Hillsborough disaster, had never played a single minute of senior football, and while Carson's experience wasn't much higher in terms of games played at first-team level he was already an England under-21 international, and was being heavily tipped for greatness. The big question for Benítez was whether he took a chance on a younger prospect like Carson, or if he should opt for a more experienced goalkeeper.

Post-Norwich, attentions were all set to turn to the FA Cup, with a Friday night third-round tie scheduled at Turf Moor against Burnley, only for the game to be called off by Mark Clattenburg, 45 minutes prior to kick-off, with supporters already descending; the velocity of a pre-match deluge caught everyone by surprise and left a small part of the pitch that had been uncovered as a quagmire, something that ground staff had hastily attempted to counteract by throwing copious amounts of sand at only to render it totally unplayable in that section.

So instead, focus shifted to the following Tuesday and the first leg of the League Cup semi-final against Watford at Anfield, where in an otherwise disjointed collective performance Gerrard scored the only goal of the game 11 minutes into the second half, laid on by Baroš, who had only been on the pitch for three minutes, the striker's comeback from his hamstring injury having been as much stop than it had been start.

Watford had enjoyed spells when they were the better team, with Gavin Mahon and Brynjar Gunnarsson taking control in midfield and Paul Devlin creating a handful of dangerous openings, before going rabbit in the headlights in the final third, unable as they were to find the composure needed to put the ball in the net. The evening ended with a subdued reaction from the home supporters, and jubilation among the 6,000-strong away section.

One of the men behind this composed rather than stubborn Watford performance was their goalkeeper, Paul Jones, on loan from Wolverhampton Wanderers and a year on from having enjoyed a short loan spell at Anfield where he was able to turn out in a couple of Premier League games, in the process fulfilling a childhood dream of playing for Liverpool.

Four days later it was the visit of Manchester United to Anfield, and for the first 20 minutes Liverpool were very much in control until Dudek, for the third season in succession, gifted a goal at home to Sir Alex Ferguson's side when failing to deal with what seemed an entirely saveable Wayne Rooney effort from 25 yards that squirmed beneath his body.

Two wildly differing Liverpool performances in one, the version before the goal and the one afterwards, saw Benítez's side became increasingly swamped in midfield after falling behind, with Roy Keane able to take advantage of Gerrard being pulled in a multitude of directions, plugging defensive gaps and pushing up to supplement a faltering attack.

Rather than a centre ground duel, Keane was able to dictate the flow of the game, balanced by the industry of Paul Scholes, while Gerrard bounced around like a bluebottle struggling with the concept of a window on a hot summer's day. Keane went on to strike Dudek's crossbar, and Liverpool's first effort on target didn't materialise until injury time, Carragher being denied by Roy Carroll. Neither Pellegrino nor Morientes had been able to make an impact on their debuts and even the sending-off of Wes Brown with just under 25 minutes remaining didn't reinvigorate the home team.

Morientes's transfer had finally been completed 48 hours prior to the Manchester United game, and while he would be a valuable figure on the domestic front, Madrid's use of him in the group stage of the Champions League had cup tied him for Europe, with the same applicable for Pellegrino who had appeared in the competition for Valencia.

From bad to worse: three days later it was back to Turf Moor for the rearranged FA Cup third round tie against Burnley and a moment of iconography with Traoré's unfortunate own goal, one which was eventually immortalised in one of the greatest Liverpool chants ever. On a blustery night, the self-inflicted only goal of the game came six minutes into the second half, and while its method was esoteric, Burnley were more than worthy of their victory.

Benítez had made a raft of changes to his line-up, with David Raven, Zak Whitbread, John Welsh, and Darren Potter all drafted in, but the balance of youth and experience jarred, with frustrations eventually leading to the 87th-minute dismissal of Núñez after a clash with the former Everton midfielder Tony Grant.

With little in the way of time to lick their wounds, Liverpool were soon heading to Southampton, although it was a trip they made at last armed with a goalkeeping reinforcement, with Carson being signed a couple of days after the defeat to Burnley.

Next to bottom of the Premier League and with just two wins from their opening 23, Harry Redknapp had been in the St Mary's hotseat for six and a half weeks yet was still awaiting his first three points. On paper a morale-boosting victory was Liverpool's to claim, but within 22 minutes they were 2-0 down, David Prutton seizing upon a return pass by Peter Crouch after Pellegrino had been caught in possession, with the compliment reversed for Southampton's second. Benítez was left to jot down notes about Crouch for future reference.

A third successive defeat for Liverpool, the closest they came to scoring was when Gerrard skimmed the crossbar, but by and large it was another sorry showing and Rory Delap was wasteful with a huge opportunity to make it 3-0 on a day when the visitors' midfield was outmanoeuvred by an opposing engine room that included the injury-ravaged former Liverpool captain Jamie Redknapp, who played a key role in Crouch's headed goal.

Premier League activities over for a difficult January, somehow Liverpool were still sat in fifth position, but were seven points away from the Champions League berths and an alarming 24 points behind the runaway leaders Chelsea. This was with just under a third of the season left to play. Before the dawning of February, Liverpool had just one more fixture to navigate, and the prize was a trip to the Millennium Stadium.

Getting to a point of desperation for some positive vibes, the next blow to the gut to wind Benítez was his declaration in the build-up to the second leg of the League Cup semi-final that Alonso might not play again before the end of the season, while the manager also had to contend with the loss of Hyypiä, who had limped out of the defeat at Southampton midway through the second half.

At Vicarage Road, just as in the first leg, and in a game of few clear-cut chances, with 13 minutes remaining Gerrard scored the only goal of the evening again, this after passing a pre-match fitness test over a niggling hamstring; yet even within a window of positivity, there was the juxtaposition of the loss of another player for the rest of the campaign, with Pongolle tearing the anterior cruciate ligament in his left knee just four minutes after his introduction as a late substitute in place of Baroš.

At the very outset of February, after a free weekend due to most other Premier League teams being involved in the fourth round of the FA Cup, Liverpool were again headed south in midweek with a Tuesday evening trip to The Valley to face Charlton Athletic. With Benítez's squad strengthened not only by the return of Hyypiä but also the first sighting of the season of Vladimír Šmicer after he had spent six months out with a knee ligament injury, there was another name to now throw into the mix, that of Anthony Le Tallec, after the early curtailing of his season-long loan at Saint-Étienne.

On the debit side, Benítez sent his team into the game without the services of suspended duo Hamann and Núñez, and when Shaun Bartlett headed home a Danny Murphy corner after 20 minutes of football during which Liverpool had made a promising start the evening could have easily followed the pattern of the defeat at home to Manchester United, with low confidence and mental fragility precipitating a struggle to absorb the blow of conceding a goal against the run of play, something which could all too feasibly have led to another loss.

Such a theory was not to occur on this occasion, however. Retaining their composure, Liverpool returned from the interval to sweep to victory, with Riise leading the charge on the left of midfield, going on to score the winning goal with ten minutes remaining, this after having earlier been denied by the frame of Dean Kiely's goal.

Reassuringly, Morientes had claimed his first goal in a Liverpool shirt with a well-taken equaliser as part of a rounded performance in which his link play was excellent, while Gerrard revelled in this collective example of what the Benítez-styled Liverpool could evolve towards. The captain also saw a fizzing effort of his own bounce back off the crossbar, seizing upon the opportunity after a fine save by Kiely from García on an evening when the Charlton goalkeeper was in an inspired mood.

Morientes was again on target four days later during the visit to Anfield of Fulham, with Liverpool running out 3-1 winners. Another show of character: when Morientes gave the home side the lead in the ninth minute, the advantage only lasted for seven minutes before Andrew Cole grabbed the equaliser. Yet, with a positive mindset, Liverpool eased to the three points with a second-half goal apiece for Hyypiä and Baroš.

A trip to Cardiff in the League Cup Final theirs, the knockout stage of the Champions League to look forward to and back-to-back wins in the Premier League obtained, climbing to within five points of fourth-placed Everton, and the addition of Morientes to his squad, with three months of the season to go, as Liverpool rolled towards mid-February there was reason for optimism as they set sail for St Andrew's to take on Birmingham City.

Caught by a Darren Anderton sucker-punch when facing Steve Bruce's side at Anfield back in November, here was the opportunity to settle a score against a team that since the turn of the year had lost five of their last six league games and been knocked out of the FA Cup in the third round. Having dropped to 14th in the Premier League table, while Birmingham were still comfortably nine points clear of the bottom three, Bruce had been concerned enough by results to make loan moves for Deportivo de La Coruña's Uruguayan international striker Walter Pandiani and Arsenal's talented yet often-troubled winger Jermaine Pennant.

Pennant had been the Notts County wonderkid who was signed for £2m as a 15-year-old by Arsène Wenger in 1999, but had struggled with the weight of expectancy at Highbury, although he had been one of the few positives for Leeds during 2003/04 when he spent the season at Elland Road on loan during their Premier League relegation campaign.

Having failed to take the fresh opportunities handed to him by Wenger at Arsenal during the first half of 2004/05, Pennant had jumped at the chance to play out the remainder of the season at Birmingham, and his presence was felt immediately when providing the assist for Pandiani to score the opening goal during the team's one solitary victory of 2005 up until now, at home to struggling Southampton ten days before the arrival of Liverpool.

Despite the chance to close the gap on Everton to just two points, Liverpool put in a frustratingly listless performance at St Andrew's in which they were outfought in midfield and stretched in wide positions, Pennant in particular giving Riise a tough afternoon in the West Midlands sleet. A 2-0 defeat with both goals scored within a seven-minute span leading up to the interval: Pandiani had netted the first, converting from the penalty spot after Hyypiä was adjudged to have fouled Emile Heskey, before a poor effort at clearing the ball by Traoré resulted in Pennant linking well with Julian Gray for the latter to grab the second.

Far too often brushed aside in key battles for the second ball, given little time to dwell on the ball with considered thought when they were in possession of it, and failing to muster an effort on target until the 90th minute, this was not the manner in which Liverpool's players should have been preparing for the first leg of the last 16 in the Champions League, with Bayer Leverkusen's visit to Anfield still a full ten days away given that another free weekend was looming due to the fifth round of the FA Cup taking place without them.

A Liverpool performance without inspiration, heart, structure, or penetration, it was 90 minutes that represented a similar shock to the system to the one that had been delivered at Southampton three weeks earlier against opponents that should have been ripe for the picking off, a Birmingham team that hadn't kept a clean sheet since Boxing Day.

With Hamann and Biščan both deployed in defensive midfield roles, often duplicating each other's duties, and Baroš playing out of position on the right, it meant that Morientes was largely isolated and shackled by Matthew Upson, the three points being meekly handed as a gift to the home team on a day when Liverpool went into the game in the knowledge that Everton had already lost at Goodison Park against Chelsea.

Left with the best part of a week and a half to think about what they had done at St Andrew's, much soul-searching was on the agenda, with Benítez staging a meeting with his players the following Monday to lay out his demands for greater consistency, and that collective responsibility had to be accepted, harder work embraced, and basic errors eliminated. Some members of the squad would have shifted more uneasily in their chairs than others.

Beyond the fallout from the loss at Birmingham, it was all about working on negating the negatives and accentuating the positives in the prolonged build-up to the arrival at Anfield of Leverkusen. On one hand, the speculation over Gerrard's future was a continuingly stubborn topic of conversation, this time his name being linked with Real Madrid, yet on the upside the January transfer window had now closed, so it would be a moot point this side of the last kick of the 2004/05 season bringing such unexpected glory with it.

Added to this, with Morientes cup-tied, the focus shifted to the positivity being projected by Baroš, who was looking forward to resuming a role through the middle. Meanwhile, although Harry Kewell had been absent for seven weeks with a groin injury, he had made an impression in his comeback in the reserves and Benítez was pleased with his attitude and increasing confidence in training, making him a possible inclusion for the first leg against Leverkusen. Le Tallec too, had been motivated in training in a bid to prove Saint-Étienne wrong in their ending of his loan spell with them four months earlier than proposed.

Almost three years on from having faced Leverkusen in the 2001/02 Champions League quarter-finals, when Liverpool came within just six minutes of an all-English semi-final against Manchester United, both teams had undergone enough significant change since for the tie not to feel overtly like a rematch as such. Both under different management, for the first leg Liverpool and Leverkusen fielded just five survivors each from the corresponding fixture at Anfield three years earlier.

New enterprise or not, and despite the suspension of their captain, Liverpool flew into Leverkusen like a team possessed, very much on point in channelling their frustrations from the Birmingham defeat and not having been able to scratch the itch with a swift follow-up game within the immediacy of the self-inflicted wound sustained at St Andrew's.

As he would also go on to be in the second leg, García was the inspiration, scorer of the opening goal and a constant thorn in the Leverkusen side. He made the breakthrough within 15 minutes when latching on to a beautifully weighted through ball from Bišćan, who was again revelling in a European night. Across the remaining 165 minutes or so of the two legs of the tie, Leverkusen were never really in contention once García found the back of the net.

Yes, Leverkusen crafted themselves some fine openings of their own during the game, yet profligacy was at play with Dimitar Berbatov the guiltiest of parties for the visitors, whereas Liverpool were ruthless in front of goal, a Riise free kick doubling their lead ten minutes

THERE ARE PLACES I REMEMBER

prior to half-time, catching Hans-Jörg Butt out at his near post when a cross rather than a shot was anticipated by the German international.

Anfield bouncing, the supporters doing their part, Liverpool were in consummate control of proceedings and had the otherwise tireless Baroš not been quite so wayward with his finishing then Benítez's side would have ended the first leg with a wider margin of lead than the two-goal advantage they eventually came away with.

Amid the flow of traffic mostly travelling towards the Leverkusen penalty area, the visitors were coherent enough to throw out the occasional counterpunch, and Dudek did pull off one excellent save midway through the second half when spectacularly tipping over a very well-struck Bernd Schneider volley, this after the Pole had already twice headed off one-on-one situations, the best of which fell to Berbatov after a defensive mix-up between Finnan and Hyypiä, only for the Bulgarian to shoot wastefully wide.

Just as he had been away to Deportivo de La Coruña in the group stage, Bišćan was again a Champions League revelation against Leverkusen, the part he played in the opening goal not only consisting of his wonderful pass but also some calm and composed weaving past Carsten Ramelow and Paul Freier to provide himself the space to create in the first place.

Increasingly frustrated, Freier and Robson Ponte picked up yellow cards that meant they would be suspended for the return leg, a fixture that Gerrard would now be available for. An evening that erred towards what could go wrong would go wrong as far as Leverkusen were concerned as in the 90th minute Hamann made it 3-0, Klaus Augenthaler's side again undone at a free kick. So close to bringing the curtain down on the perfect night's work from Benítez's men, just seconds later Dudek's concentration momentarily slipped when spilling a harmless enough bobbling effort from Berbatov, gifting a loose ball that the substitute Franca was swift to pounce upon to make the scoreline 3-1. An unfortunate end to a magnificent evening for Liverpool; instead of heading to the BayArena safe in the knowledge that Leverkusen would have to score three without reply just to take the tie into extra time, now a 2-0 victory for the 2001/02 runners-up would be enough to take them into the quarter-finals on the away goals rule. For Benítez and his players, to panic or not to panic – that would be the question in Germany.

With little in the way of time for critical introspection, Benítez was quick to point out that Dudek had made some crucial contributions prior to his late mistake, and it was instead toward the impending League Cup Final that the manager turned his focus, with the trip to the Millennium Stadium coming just five days later.

Not an entirely smooth build-up to the final against Chelsea, and still battling to change the general mindset of his squad at times, Benítez had found himself having to take his captain to task over comments he had made regarding his thoughts on Liverpool's chances of winning the Champions League, with Gerrard's pragmatic view being amplified in the press as defeatism, something the player felt hadn't been presented in the manner he intended.

Regardless, with Chelsea still deemed to be his most likely summer destination and Gerrard's insistence that he would assess his future at the end of the season, combined with José Mourinho's unabashed admiration of him, along with the deep pockets of Roman Abramovich and the kingmaker string-pulling of Peter Kenyon, it meant that the game itself was playing second fiddle to the kitchen sink drama element of Gerrard's future.

Amid this flux, Gerrard was not the only Liverpool midfielder whose future was open to debate, with Hamann uncommitted on a proposed one-year contract extension for the 2005/06 season and seemingly happy to weigh up alternative options alongside considering the invite to prolong his stay at Anfield for another season. Added to this, despite his impressive Champions League cameos, Bišćan was on the countdown to the expiration of his contract in the summer too, with little in the way of talk over an extension being offered.

To Cardiff, Liverpool and their supporters headed, to a stadium and city that had become the new Anfield South during the four years since the 2001 League Cup Final had become the first major English football domestic showpiece event to be played away from the old Wembley since its closure in 2000 for what would go on to be an unexpectedly protracted rebuild.

Chelsea were fresh off the back of losing 2-1 to Barcelona at the Camp Nou in the Champions League, and having been tipped out of the FA Cup by Newcastle prior to that, with an added altercation for Mourinho in the tunnel in the Catalan capital, the Stamford Bridge supremo was busy fostering a siege mentality for his team in the days before the game, while the more measured Benítez was content to keep it to analysing how to win the trophy with the ball at his players' feet rather than be drawn into attempted mind games.

Nine of the starting 11 that had faced Leverkusen were in from the kick-off at Cardiff, with the unsurprising returns of Gerrard and Morientes meaning that Biščan and Baroš made way, the latter in particular valid to feel aggrieved in missing out. A backhanded compliment to the Czech striker, Benítez's inability to find room for Baroš did at least indicate a step in the right direction with regards to the strengthening of the pool of players he could choose from.

As perfect a start as possible for Liverpool: a beautiful cross from Morientes and there was Riise powering a volley past Petr Čech with only 45 seconds having elapsed, from which 78 minutes of Benítez-plotted resilience followed, until the Gerrard narrative proved too strong an element to remain a subplot as he inadvertently flicked a Paulo Ferreira free kick beyond a stranded Dudek for an undeserved Chelsea equaliser which bounced in off the post.

Liverpool's defence had been well organised, and they had suffered no significant first-half scares, although Chelsea did come out for the second half with greater purpose with Dudek being forced into an excellent double save in the 54th minute, first denying Eiður Guðjohnsen and then William Gallas's follow up, yet between these opportunities and the fortuitous nature of the eventual equaliser, Liverpool conceding a goal seemed increasingly unlikely.

Hamann had even forced Čech into a crucial second-half save of his own, and three minutes prior to the equaliser Gerrard had been denied a goal by a last-ditch tackle by Ferreira; an alternative, positive outcome to the final was rapidly evaporating for Liverpool, with the blow of Gerrard's own goal beginning a snowball effect in which the game would escape their previously steely grasp.

Within the span of time between Chelsea's equaliser and the end of the initial 90 minutes, Mourinho's team had the opportunity to win with Damian Duff being denied by a smart save from Dudek as the weight of pressure on the Liverpool defence dramatically increased in velocity, Benítez's side doing well to maintain their resolve and take the final into extra time.

Undeniably, the second half had been infinitely more testing for Liverpool than the first half had been, even before the equaliser materialised, with Kewell lasting less than an hour before being replaced by Núñez, while the loss of the impressive Traoré further upset the chemistry of the midfield, with Riise forced to drop into left-back, the in-form Norwegian having been a clear threat higher up on the left.

As an attacking threat, Liverpool had gradually been neutralised, yet Chelsea were reliant upon a huge slice of luck to break the lock that Benítez had strategically placed on his defence, with this stubbornness set to bring the League Cup back to Anfield for the eighth time until fate dealt its cruel blow for Gerrard.

Yet things could still have been different; five minutes prior to the leveller, Benítez had played the last card from his collection of substitutes with Baroš replacing Morientes, and the man who had missed out on a place in the starting line-up could have won it in the final minute only for the chance to come and then go without being taken.

Overwhelmed in extra time, within minutes of the restart Didier Drogba had struck the post with a diving header, and momentum had definitively swung, although Benítez's side didn't buckle until the second minute of the second period of the extra 30 minutes, Drogba finally making his power felt by scoring from close-range after a long throw by the future Liverpool right-back Glen Johnson.

Drogba, like Duff, had been successfully blotted out of the game up until this point, with Carragher and Finnan allowing neither of them much in the way of space and time on the ball in what had been a masterclass of defending and control, leading Mourinho to regularly alter his angles of attack only to see them repelled, Guðjohnsen having replaced Jiří Jarošík after just 45 minutes, Duff being switched to the right, and a tweak in formation from 4-3-3 to 4-2-4 all speaking of a growing desperation until Chelsea stumbled their way to parity.

Five minutes beyond Drogba giving Chelsea the lead, Mateja Kežman was on hand to score their third, another close-range strike, after a Guðjohnsen cross had bounced off Dudek. The final was essentially won and lost not through Gerrard's own goal but by Chelsea's greater quality of substitutes, with Kežman, Guðjohnsen, and Johnson all making key contributions from the bench, whereas for Liverpool the introductions of Núñez, Bišćan, and Baroš had not shifted the direction of play in the same manner, although Núñez did outjump Čech to head home for 3-2 and offer his team a glimmer of hope during the last seven minutes.

It was not to be for Liverpool, however, and it was the blue end of the Millennium Stadium that was celebrating at the final whistle, although Chelsea's manager was forced to do his own rejoicing in the dressing room after being sent from the touchline having indulged in a lack of class in the wake of his team's equaliser, opting for shushing gestures rather than living the moment, actions that were arguably a compliment in disguise, a release of pent-up frustrations over how the game was panning out before fortune favoured him.

In terms of Liverpool's starting 11 up against Chelsea's, Benítez's side had more than matched their opponents up until the equaliser, and solace could be taken in that an extraordinary turn of events had literally deflected the outcome on to a different path compared to the one Liverpool had dictated for 79 minutes.

While defeat in Cardiff was a painful experience, it was important to look to the positives too, and Gerrard had dominated midfield during the first half, Carragher, Finnan, and Traoré had all stifled the Chelsea players they were detailed to shadow, Hyypiä had been the equal to the aerial bombardment that Mourinho's team had been reduced to, and Dudek had been concentration personified.

However, beyond half-time, those in red who were operating in Liverpool's final third had become increasingly isolated as the pressure on Benítez's defence grew and grew, meaning that the lack of the injured Alonso was ultimately pivotal; Liverpool's had been a team shorn of a man in possession of the kind of calm assurance that wins trophies amid maelstroms such as the one that escalated at the Millennium Stadium, especially on a day when a creative hub such as Kewell had struggled to impose himself, leaving the burden of linking midfield and attack predominantly on the shoulders of García. It was doubly galling that Alonso's absence had been caused by one of Chelsea's celebrating players.

Losing the League Cup Final had been a significant blow, and without a midweek fixture, Liverpool had had to wait six days before they were handed their first opportunity to work their frustrations out of their system as they headed back into Premier League action at St James' Park against Graeme Souness's Newcastle United.

If Benítez was banking on a positive response then he was to be greatly disappointed, as a poor game was settled by an outstanding free kick by Laurent Robert 20 minutes from time, a goal that was entirely at odds with the general quality of proceedings but one which was beautifully struck from 25 yards, eluding the grasp of Carson, who had been brought in for his Liverpool debut, with Dudek sat on the bench nursing a badly bruised shin sustained against Chelsea.

No Dudek, but also without the services of Traoré, Hamann, Kewell, and Morientes, to go alongside the longer-term absentees of Kirkland, Josemi, Alonso, Djibril Cissé, Sinama Pongolle, and Mellor, on Tyneside in came not only Carson but also Pellegrino, Bišćan, the now disgruntled Baroš, and in Šmicer a player who was starting a Liverpool game for the first time in ten months.

Another domestic defeat absorbed, this had been Liverpool's first Premier League outing for three weeks and they now sat eight points behind fourth-placed Everton; obtaining a win had been absolutely necessary toward what were now drifting hopes of qualifying for the following season's Champions League, yet drive and inspiration from the captain were not on the menu.

An anonymous performance from Gerrard, the type of afternoon where the narrative for the articles of journalists in attendance was easily written, it meant that the build-up to the looming second leg of the last-16 of the Champions League away to Leverkusen would be themed in terms of a lack of heart for the fight to drag Liverpool back to pre-eminence for Gerrard, and that his future likely lay away from Anfield.

James Lawton of *The Independent* was particularly withering in his view, and while conceding the talents possessed by Gerrard, it was his want to question how often he had exploited them for Liverpool throughout the 2004/05 season. In some respects it was a fair question to pose, yet here was a player carrying the weight of personal and collective responsibility on his broad shoulders without much in the way of reliable assistance.

At Newcastle, the unimpeachable Carragher was again in belligerent mood, marshalling the backline magnificently, while García was the creator of any threat Liverpool managed to pose to Shay Given's gloves, but the constantly revolving door nature of those around Gerrard in midfield was clearly doing the captain no favours at all. Confidence ebbing away, he missed the only chance of true purpose that fell his team's way, deep into stoppage time.

Conversely, away from Liverpool's domestic difficulties, the Champions League was representing something of a safe haven, an environment where Benítez and his squad could play to their strengths, away from the demolition derby ethos of the parochial variant of the game in England. In defeating Leverkusen during the first leg, Liverpool had been the only Premier League team to pick off a victory across the first wave of last-16 fixtures, with Arsenal and Chelsea losing in Munich and Barcelona respectively, while Manchester United had been beaten at Old Trafford by Milan.

Flying in the face of recent results, Benítez was brimming with confidence ahead of the trip to Germany, insisting in his pre-travel press conference that with Porto and Monaco having contested the 2004 final then it wasn't the impossibility many thought it to be that Liverpool could reach the 2005 showpiece. Furthermore, he was swift to point out that the 3-1 first-leg advantage his team harboured was a healthy one to be taking to

North Rhine-Westphalia, and that whoever they might face beyond the last 16, should they return to Merseyside with a place in the quarter-finals, would have to go up against the might of Anfield on a European night.

Since their loss at Anfield, Leverkusen had failed to win either of their intervening two Bundesliga fixtures, drawing once and losing once, their most recent outing having been a 1-0 defeat away to Hamburger SV, this having followed a 1-1 draw at home to VfB Stuttgart in which they had conceded a late penalty. With Leverkusen's own mounting injury issues being exacerbated by suspensions, Benítez was right to feel bullish about Liverpool's prospects.

With Kewell having withdrawn from the squad before the flight set off, it meant that Gerrard was handed a freer roaming remit at the BayArena, supplemented by a twin defensive central midfield pairing of Hamann and Bišćan, with García operating a key role when drifting in from wide on the right and into central areas while Baroš was asked to pull the Leverkusen defence in all directions with his running.

Within three minutes, Baroš was testing Butt, who had to drop low to make an excellent reaction stop, and not long afterwards the same player had a reasonable shout for a penalty waved away, yet despite these near misses, nerves were not at play and a deserved lead was gained in the 28th minute when García flicked the ball past the Leverkusen goalkeeper from a Gerrard corner, Butt having made a fine save from a thunderous drive by the number eight.

Dissaray in the Leverkusen ranks, and soon they suffered the blow of losing the attacking potency of Dimitar Berbatov to injury, replaced by Andriy Voronin, and while the disorientation of that change and the opening goal was still working its way through the system of the home team, García struck again as yet another Gerrard corner found its way to the former Barcelona man's feet in the penalty area, this time via a flick-on by Bišćan.

So much having been made of the potential relevancy of the late goal that Dudek had gifted Leverkusen at Anfield, with just over half an hour played in the second leg Liverpool would now have to concede five goals without replay across the last hour of the game in order to throw away their place in the quarter-finals.

Effervescent in his performance, García should have had a ten-minute hat-trick to his name only to be denied by the reactions of Butt, while Gerrard was a blur of motion, demonstrating the full range of his passing repertoire on an evening when he empathically answered his critics, both those in the press box and closer to home.

Left to throw caution to the wind in the second half, Leverkusen upped their game but this simply played into the hands of Liverpool who regularly hit on the break, Baroš contriving to miskick when presented with one golden opportunity in front of goal, before making amends in the 67th minute, taking advantage of a kind bounce of the ball off Clemens Fritz after a searching pass from Riise to break through on Butt, who he beat with a low shot.

Presented with an unfamiliar luxury of the job being done with plenty to spare, Benítez was able to withdraw Carragher and Hamann from the fray after Liverpool's third goal, protecting both players who were sat a yellow card away from suspension for the first leg of the quarter-final, bringing Núñez and Welsh into play, while he was also able to hand Šmicer another 30 minutes of action on an evening when Warnock excelled at left-back, allowing Riise to push up to cover the gap left empty by Kewell's unavailability. The perfect evening – not even Jacek Krzynówek's late consolation for Leverkusen could take any shine off the Reds' performance.

In the away section of the BayArena, 2,000 Liverpool supporters sang in praise of their team and revelled in the added joy of having been able to enjoy a stein of two in the local bars, watching on as Manchester United toppled out of the tournament at the San Siro, while on the same night that Liverpool were claiming their place among the eight quarter-finalists, Arsenal were making their exit at Highbury.

This had been a reaffirming trip for Liverpool's supporters to Germany, and over in Köln on the eve of the game Benítez unwittingly cemented his relationship with the travelling Kop when he swung open the doors of the Jameson Distillery Pub in the company of first-team coach Alex Miller, in search of somewhere that was showing Chelsea's game against Barcelona. Timing their arrival to perfection, it wasn't long before the bar erupted in further delight as on one screen Hernán Crespo planted the ball past Manchester

United goalkeeper Roy Carroll, ending their Champions League hopes.

To Benítez's surprise, he had been confronted by the sight of roughly 100 Liverpool supporters, who were even more stunned to see him, embracing his arrival as a man of the people, whether it had been his intention or not. For half an hour or so he posed for photos and accepted every warm bear hug, enthusiastic handshake, and slap on the back, as more and more fans across the city centre caught wind of what was going on and poured into the bar to join the party.

A watermark 24 hours for Benítez; something had most definitely awoken within this sleepwalking giant of a club, and an enduring connection between manager and supporters had been made.

Chapter Eleven

Amicizia? *La Vecchia Signora* Gives the Cold Shoulder

BASKING IN the glow of overcoming Bayer Leverkusen and obtaining themselves a place in the quarter-finals of the Champions League, supporters and players alike were beginning to dream that the perceived impossible was actually possible after all. However, the number crunchers at William Hill HQ still weren't sold on the prospect of Liverpool becoming the champions of Europe, classing them no more than seventh favourites of the remaining eight teams and offering odds on them winning the tournament at a tempting 10/1.

In a post-match navel-gazing piece for *The Times*, George Caulkin quoted a trio of Liverpool players about the club's prospects and the intricacies of Rafael Benítez's coaching methods, with Jamie Carragher stating, 'I'm sure we'll be considered one of the outsiders in the last eight, and probably rightly so, because there are a lot of teams left in who are winning trophies and titles in their own countries, but the best teams don't always win the Champions League – anything can happen.'

While Carragher was pragmatic in his opinion yet also happy to explore the prospect that the expected narrative isn't always the one that delivers the punchline, others were more ebullient in their appraisals of the situation, with Steve Finnan certainly feeling the prize could be Liverpool's when musing, 'Of course we can do what Porto did. Nobody expected them to win it, but they did. There's no reason why we can't go all the way. Why can't we win it?'

Finnan wasn't alone in his synopsis either, with Luis García claiming, 'If Porto can win it, then so can we. In football, many unpredictable things happen every season.' Yet the comparisons to Porto's victory of 2003/04 didn't exactly draw direct parallels to Liverpool's situation of 2004/05. José Mourinho's success had been built upon rigid organisation and a settled squad, and the galvanising of a team that lost only twice in winning the Primeira Liga title, while they also narrowly lost out to Benfica in the final of the Taça de Portugal.

Yes, the 2003/04 Porto were very much the Champions League outsiders who went on to lift the trophy, just as Liverpool were one of the 2004/05 outsiders, but that is pretty much where the similarities ended. For Benítez and his players, the target might well have been the same as what Porto had successfully aimed for a year earlier, but the method and the landscape Liverpool would have to pick their way through to do it was of an entirely different terrain.

A peculiar set of ingredients were at play for Liverpool, with their domestic inconsistencies deriving from the avalanche of injuries they had had to cope with, alongside the personal and professional learning curve that Benítez was on during his first season within the culture shock that was English football. Unable to sustain meaningful Premier League momentum at any stage of the campaign, the juxtaposition of reaching the quarter-finals of the Champions League and being able to daydream of glory despite such domestic difficulties spoke loudly of the Jekyll and Hyde nature of what was unfolding.

In the last 16 Liverpool had comprehensively brushed Leverkusen aside home and away, and giving even more cause for optimism, Carragher went on to offer insights into the meticulous nature of the project that Benítez was building at Anfield when he said, 'We probably do more tactical work now than I have done with any manager in my career.'

Whether they went on to succeed or fall short in the Champions League in Benítez's first year with the club, it was becoming increasingly evident that Liverpool were in possession of a manager who would leave no stone unturned in his search for the knowledge to give his team the very best chance to succeed, to be able to throw their hat confidently into the ring for the biggest prizes.

As Liverpool and their supporters took their leave of the BayArena after the second leg of the Leverkusen game, they were left with a nine-day wait to find out what lay ahead of them in the quarter-final draw, with the added caveat that the draw for the semi-final would also be made, creating with it the type of bracket draw that tennis lovers were more familiar with as opposed to football supporters.

In the meantime, it was back to Premier League duties with the impending midweek visit to Anfield of Mark Hughes's Blackburn Rovers for a game that was taking place seven days beyond the trip to North Rhine-Westphalia, Liverpool having been afforded a weekend off due to the FA Cup quarter-finals taking place, the team from Ewood Park having obtained themselves a semi-final spot with a 1-0 victory at home to Leicester City.

By rights, with home advantage, a week to prepare, and up against opponents that had played at the weekend and were water-treading in the bottom half of the Premier League, this was a golden opportunity for Liverpool to get back to winning ways domestically, with their two most recent outings in the competition having ended in defeats away to Birmingham City and Newcastle United.

Refreshed and renewed by their Champions League progress, Benítez's side had the chance to close the gap on fourth-placed Everton to five points, yet Blackburn were to provide a stubborn resistance, grinding out a goalless draw that did Liverpool no favours at all in their aspirations of a top-four finish.

Conversely to Liverpool's recent fortunes in the league, Blackburn had won their previous two games, with the second of those victories being picked up over on the other side of Stanley Park, at Goodison against Everton. A team of few goals finding the back of the net at either end, a stalemate shouldn't have come as a massive surprise against Hughes's side, yet it didn't ease frustrations as Liverpool mediocrity was repelled by the solidity of Blackburn's defence.

On an evening upon which neither Jerzy Dudek nor Brad Friedel had a save of note to make, Hughes flooded his midfield and deployed his defence deep, with Aaron Mokoena patrolling the minimal space between the two lines, strangulating the minimal gap in which García, Steven Gerrard, and Vladimír Šmicer were permitted to create, thus leaving Fernando Morientes and Milan Baroš without much in the way of a supply line of chances, not that there was much urgency of endeavour and invention from those playing in red.

With little in the way of positives for Benítez to take solace from, a first start of the season for Šmicer lasted for just 45 minutes before he was replaced by John Arne Riise after the interval, while Harry Kewell had been highly vocal earlier in the day over questions that had been raised over his desire and willingness to play.

Lumbering away from their travails against Blackburn, all attentions now turned to the looming Champions League draw, and 48 hours beyond that the 201st Merseyside derby lay in wait, a game that Anfield would be playing host to, and the chance for Liverpool to pull to within four points of their neighbours in the race for fourth place.

In Nyon, into UEFA's Perspex orb went Liverpool alongside five other clubs that had previously been champions of Europe, plus two that had never reached such heights before, in what was an unseeded draw with no restrictions on teams facing opponents from their own nation. With the bookmakers giving Benítez's side only better odds than PSV Eindhoven to win the Champions League, Matt Dickinson of *The Times* opined that Liverpool would represent a plum draw when summing up Chelsea's prospects moving forward, in a field of contenders that also included Milan, Internazionale, Juventus, Bayern Munich, and Olympique Lyonnais.

Being unconsidered as a threat was to suit Liverpool down to the ground, and the draw – which pitted Benítez and his players against Fabio Capello and Juventus – meant that the focus was skewed towards the events of 20 years earlier more than it was on matters of the pitch across the two and a half weeks that sat between the draw being made and the first leg kicking off at Anfield.

Ironically, on the very morning of the draw being made, the Association of the Families of Heysel Victims had called upon UEFA to organise a game between the two clubs to mark the anniversary of the Brussels tragedy, a friendly that they hoped could mark a new beginning in relations between the red side of Merseyside and the black and white half of Turin. The pairing of Liverpool and Juventus in the quarter-finals ensured there would be two games, with something far more tangible than cordiality at stake.

Both clubs were quick in their attempts to diffuse the potential for volatility, with Rick Parry, the Liverpool chief executive, although unwilling to speculate on the finer details of how they would mark the occasion at Anfield, clear in his view that there would be a ceremony of some form and that it would be low-key and dignified with supporters consulted on how to proceed. Juventus's director of marketing and communications, Romy Gai, was keen to state that the two clubs had long had a positive relationship which had stemmed from the very immediacy of the Heysel tragedy.

No concerted time to linger on thoughts of Juventus; attention had to be switched to the visit of Everton where anything less than victory would surely mean a top-four spot would realistically be beyond Liverpool, with only eight league games remaining once this one had been navigated. Victory would be Liverpool's, but not without drama needing to be dealt with to get there.

Two goals to the good within 32 minutes, forced into all three substitutions before half-time, and having to stagger over the finish line with ten men, there was a little bit of everything for Liverpool to deal with in this one, including an injured García playing through the pain barrier throughout the entirety of the second half after receiving a painful kick to the ankle.

Stephen Warnock departed before Liverpool took the lead, with a damaged ankle, to be followed by Hamann and Morientes with knee and thigh problems respectively, within three minutes of one another just before the interval, losses that were exacerbated further by the needless dismissal of Baroš in the 77th minute for going in with studs bared to Alan Stubbs's knee.

A physical rather than dirty game, one which was embodied by the relish of central midfield battle between Gerrard and Lee Carsley, plus the central defensive mastery of Carragher, it was Liverpool who flew into action from the off and the only surprise was that it took them until the 26th minute to break the deadlock, when a Gerrard effort from a rolled Hamann free kick was struck low, avoiding the blocking efforts of four runners from the Everton wall, the ball arrowing to the left of Nigel Martyn who reacted late as it nestled into the Kop end net.

Excellent for Everton all season, and one of the biggest reasons that David Moyes's side were in pole position for Champions League qualification, Martyn was to experience a hugely uncomfortable afternoon, beaten again six minutes later when caught out by a dipping 30-yard shot from Morientes that the former England international goalkeeper initially claimed with both hands, only to release his grasp as he fell backwards towards his own goal line, pushing the ball up and on to his crossbar from where the alert García was quick to pounce on the rebound.

A wonderfully driven first half from Liverpool, the concerns lay in the prospect of them reappearing for the second half with only ten players given that García limped down the tunnel, this with all three substitutions having already been made, and the expected Everton response to revolve around a route-one approach, something that was accentuated by the introduction of James Beattie from the bench for the restart and the throwing on of Duncan Ferguson ten minutes later.

Carragher was imperious, however, this without the presence of Sami Hyypiä alongside him, partnered instead – for a second successive game – by the struggling

Mauricio Pellegrino, the pair offering up a rich defiance of the predictable aerial bombardment that came, apart from Tim Cahill's 82nd minute goal that gave the visitors late hope of pulling a rabbit from the hat during the mad dash to the final whistle.

After so many domestic setbacks across the span of the season, the let-off at the end blew so many cobwebs away, with even Benítez feeling compelled to take to the pitch to embrace his players and to enjoy the adulation of the Kop for at least a snapshot moment, forgetting briefly about the renewal of an escalating injury crisis that was threatening to leave him without a striker to call upon for the games ahead, resulting in post-match questions over whether or not he might be tempted to recall El Hadji Diouf from his season-long loan at Bolton Wanderers. This despite the Senegalese international facing his own three-match ban.

Injuries aside, the only bone of contention for Liverpool was the rush of blood from Baroš in earning himself a fully deserved red card, with Benítez not even offering his striker a side-eye glance as the player made for the tunnel and his early bath on an afternoon when he had twice squandered one-on-one situations with Martyn, wasting opportunities to put the game way beyond Everton, and instead, combined to his sending off, gifting them a late route back into a match they had no right to take anything from.

With the stricken García battling through to the final whistle, Liverpool effectively finished with nine men, and Gerrard was hard pressed to conceal his annoyance with

Baroš during his post-match interviews, lamenting the missed chances more than the dismissal.

Frustratingly, with the late-March international break now ahead, Liverpool were left with a 13-day wait until taking to the pitch again, although the break did at least allow a couple of wounds to heal with García and Morientes fit and available for selection for the visit of Bolton, who had temporarily leapfrogged Benítez's side into fifth place prior to the Merseyside derby victory.

During the international break, a repentant Baroš apologised for his moment of madness, the realisation of where his three-match domestic ban would leave his team-mates belatedly dawning, while in other unsettling terms Benítez found himself being quoted behind only Fabio Capello by the bookmakers in the list of likely contenders to replace the hugely under pressure Vanderlei Luxemburgo, who had lost three of his last six league fixtures at the helm of Real Madrid.

Added to this, the turbulence over the composition of Benítez's Liverpool squad going beyond the summer of 2005 refused to quell, as along with the continual rumble over Gerrard's future VfB Stuttgart were the latest Bundesliga club to be linked to a summer move for the soon to be out of contract Hamann, while the now French international midfielder Alou Diarra, on a season-long loan with Lens, was beginning to play hardball on his desire for a permanent move away from Liverpool having spent three successive campaigns out on loan since his summer 2002 arrival from Bayern Munich.

Welcoming back the players he had nervously waved off on international duty, in the build-up to the visit of Bolton, along with an almost clean bill of health being reported for all who had been away on their World Cup qualifying travels, Benítez was able to project another nugget of positivity when divulging that it was no longer an impossibly that Djibril Cissé could return to action before the end of the season, this in itself being an extra bonus to go alongside Xabi Alonso working his way back to fitness too.

Going into the game, Sam Allardyce's team had suddenly made the race for fourth place a three-way fight, and with Everton now looking vulnerable, having taken just 11 points from the last 33 on offer the meeting with Bolton was now as crucial to Liverpool's hopes of a top-four finish as the clash with Moyes's side had been.

Not a pretty afternoon by any footballing means, Liverpool had to ride their luck at times with Finnan twice clearing off the goal line, from Stelios Giannakopoulos and Kevin Davies, Ricardo Gardner being wasteful with a header after a fine cross by Gary Speed, while Kevin Nolan and Jay-Jay Okocha were denied by excellent stops from Scott Carson, the teenager deputising for the only partially fit Jerzy Dudek, who was nursing a groin strain. Bolton were indulging in a collective profligacy that was punished by Igor Biščan's late winning goal, the ball arriving at the Croat after fine link play between Gerrard and Djimi Traoré.

With unintended irony, Allardyce was unable to appreciate the familiarity, in reverse, of a team being mugged off for three points, lamenting after the game that the least his Bolton side could have expected was a draw from an Anfield afternoon that they indeed widely dominated, before bringing into question the integrity of the referee Steve Bennett, with the Bolton manager being quoted by James Lawson, in *The Independent*, 'We were the better team for most of the game. But it's difficult to win when you have a foul count of 19 to five against you. Maybe Steve Bennett read the paper.'

Allardyce's final riposte of his tirade had revolved around pre-match comments by Benítez, which had suggested Bolton's physical approach was akin to a team playing by their own set of rules, and with similar sentiments having been aired by José Mourinho earlier in the season it was a bristling Allardyce who floated the theory that the mounting criticisms were maybe a sign that he was becoming a better manager than his detractors were.

Given that Everton stumbled to a 1-0 defeat away to West Bromwich Albion 24 hours later, Liverpool had drawn to within just one point of their neighbours with seven games left to play, and the smart money was now on Benítez's side to soon overtake them for fourth place in the battle for the final Champions League spot.

With Liverpool's domestic matters looking healthier than they had done all season long, attentions now turned back to the Champions League and the visit to Anfield of Juventus for the first leg of the quarter-final, a game that came with two very different spotlights cast upon it, with the on-pitch footballing challenge set to be of a high-octane nature while the weight of a painful history between the two clubs and the events of the 1985 European Cup Final was absolutely unavoidable.

Both clubs having rightly been criticised across the two decades since that fateful Brussels night for their consistently muted acknowledgements of the tragedy, there was no lack of effort by the contemporary custodians of Liverpool and Juventus to belatedly right some of the wrongs ahead of the first leg, with a wide-ranging line-up of events having been organised both by official and unofficial means.

All flights into John Lennon Airport from Italy were greeted by civic dignitaries, the city centre was decked out in Italian favours, an organised match between supporters of both teams was played out on the afternoon of the game at the Liverpool Academy complex, a special brochure was produced for visiting Juventus fans that included an apology and consolatory messages, a pre-match presentation of a plaque was made which proclaimed 'In Memory and Friendship' and was delivered to the away section of the Anfield Road end, a gesture that was overseen by Phil Neal, Ian Rush, and Michel Platini, a banner was paraded by Liverpool supporters that bared the 39 names of those who died at the Heysel Stadium, the front page of that day's *Liverpool Echo* having done likewise, while a mosaic was arranged on the Kop which read 'Amicizia', translated as friendship.

With a period of reflection prior to kick-off added into the mix, it all made for a well thought-out olive branch, but understandably many of the visitors from

Turin and elsewhere across Italy who had descended upon Merseyside in the name of their support of Juventus were unwilling to accept it, with a sizeable proportion turning their back, and extending the middle finger in response, while many others applauded the efforts.

After all of the required preliminaries had been dealt with, the football itself took most by surprise, no more so than the visitors, who were blown away during the early exchanges by the incredible powerplay of Liverpool who stunningly shot into a 2-0 lead, this against opponents who had conceded only twice across the span of the eight Champions League games that had brought them to this point since the outset of the group stages.

For the first 45 minutes it was Liverpool, rather than Juventus, who played like the team embossed with a glittering array of the good and the great of world football in all departments, rather than the team that was a pic'n'mix collective of class acts, misfits, and the occasionally unremarkable.

While Capello could call upon a litany of the finest players money could buy, with Gianluigi Buffon marshalling a defence that was manned by Fabio Cannavaro, Lilian Thuram, Jonathan Zebina, and Gianluca Zambrotta, each providing a usually solid foundation for an uncompromising but flexible midfield of Mauro Camoranesi, Emerson, Manuele Blasi, and Pavel Nedvěd, who in turn had the job to keep the supply lines to Zlatan Ibrahimović and Alessandro Del Piero fluid, here was Benítez opting to persevere with Carson in goal ahead of Dudek, and for good measure throwing in Le Tallec for his first start in a Liverpool shirt for 14 months.

All logic pointed towards a difficult night ahead for Liverpool but with Hyypiä reinstated in central defence alongside Carragher, Gerrard afforded a roaming remit thanks to the discipline of Bišćan, Riise playing in his stronger position on the left of midfield thanks to the inclusion of Traoré at left-back, Finnan continuing to link excellently on the right with García, and Le Tallec providing the link between midfield and attack to the restored Baroš, who although suspended domestically was available for Champions League duties, Benítez had managed to mould a beautifully balanced starting line-up with the added bonus of naming Alonso among his substitutes.

A Gerrard corner, a García flick on, and it was Hyypiä who opened the scoring, popping up at the back post with a finish that any self-respecting striker would be proud to call his own, this after Benítez had navigated so much of his first season in charge without the regular presence of any one individual striker and instead having to opt one in as another would drop out. Anfield embraced the bedlam as the ball hit the back of the net, and 15 minutes later it was multiplied when García made it 2-0 with an astonishing looping effort from distance that beat Buffon all ends up, having been laid on by Le Tallec.

It was a dream start for Liverpool which flew in the face of the expected convention that Juventus would represent a bridge too far for Benítez and his team, and by way of a warning that the visitors would not lie dormant all night, at the other end Ibrahimović struck Carson's post within one minute of García's goal, and soon enough the 19-year-old goalkeeper was denying Del Piero with an excellent save on the half-hour when turning a low shot around the post after a fine through ball by the up until now subdued Nedvěd.

Beyond this short flurry of endeavour by Juventus, Liverpool were then never compellingly threatened again as the game made its way towards half-time, with the first 15 minutes of the second half following a similar pattern although neither were the home team in a mood to overstretch themselves in pursuit of a third goal, at least if it meant leaving their defence vulnerable to a counter-punch.

With Capello left frustrated by events, beyond the interval he brought on the veteran Gianluca Pessotto in place of Blasi, and just after the hour he withdrew Del Piero, the latter switch being a once unthinkable proposition for the team in the black and white stripes and certainly something that would rarely have occurred under Marcello Lippi's two reigns, with the half-fit French international striker David Trezeguet being introduced for the last 30 minutes.

Within one minute of Trezeguet's arrival Juventus were very much back in the tie, but not in the manner anyone anticipated, as a Zambrotta cross was met towards the back post by the head of Cannavaro from where it bounced off the turf and agonisingly over the misshaped Carson into the Anfield Road end net.

Carson's misjudgement was similar in effect to the one that Dudek had seen go past him towards the end of the first leg against Bayer Leverkusen, except the Englishman was left with far more thinking time in this game before the final whistle was to arrive than Dudek had in the previous round. Yet aside from his error for Cannavaro's goal, the young goalkeeper had been alert to everything, but it still would have been a relief to him that Juventus seemed to take their foot off the accelerator as if content to return to Turin with the one away goal, and no more conceded at their end for Buffon.

In front of Carson, Carragher was again the defensive kingpin, and it was he who snuffed out an Ibrahimović cross that seemed destined for the dangerously positioned Trezeguet for what was the only significant threat on Carson's net beyond Cannavaro's fortuitous strike, and as the game ended there was a sweet and sour flavour in the air.

Off the pitch, Liverpool as a club and a city had done all it could to roll out the welcome mat for its roughly even mix of accepting and militantly unforgiving visitors, while on the pitch Benítez's side had proved they were a match for any opposition in the Champions League, with the electrified atmosphere from the stands playing a vital role too. Yes, the away goal conceded was unfortunate and potentially damaging, but the Reds had given themselves something precious to protect in the second leg, and the belief that they could do it too.

What followed was an eight-day sense of purgatory in anxious anticipation of the second leg at the Stadio Delle

Alpi, firstly over how matters would unfold in Turin for the travelling Liverpool supporters and secondly how events would pan out on the pitch, with a place in the semi-finals within touching distance.

Obvious concerns surrounded the prospect of revenge attacks on those making the trip to Piedmont, and even some corners of the Italian media were withering about the negative reactions that some Juventus supporters had displayed at Anfield, with *Gazzetta dello Sport* declaring Liverpool's efforts to have been 'An embrace that died against a wall of indifference', while *La Stampa* opined, 'At the festival of friendship, ignorance wins.'

Within this, there was no moral high ground to be claimed. Turin and the families of the victims had every right to be angry as a community about the horrors of Heysel, but the pantomime of professional ultras hijacking their pain as a call to arms was as damaging to their cause as the blind eye that not only Liverpool, but Juventus themselves, and UEFA had unremittingly turned for two decades.

Met with indifference or not, the club and the city itself had done the right thing in offering the hand of friendship and an unequivocal apology, and the most important thing was any solace at all that was gained by those who still suffered the first-hand reverberations of Heysel, not what the loudest voices and most visible figures thought about it on their behalf.

From a Liverpool perspective, it was all about accepting the blunt reality that those who entered Section Z from Section X in the Heysel Stadium were responsible for the deaths of 39 human beings, regardless of what negligent stepping stones UEFA and the Belgian authorities allowed to be navigated, in order for such a landscape to be even remotely possible.

It was the only genuine way of moving forward, and such enlightenment was certainly not lost on Terry Wilson, one of the 14 Liverpool supporters who were eventually deported, charged, convicted, and sentenced to time in prison in Belgium for the parts they played in the tragedy, a man who took it upon himself to travel to Turin, where he met with Otello Lorentini, a figure who helped set up the Association for the Families of Heysel Victims, a man who lost his son, Roberto, on that terrible night, somebody who fought battles for decades with Juventus for them to acknowledge what happened, rather than to continue brushing it under the carpet. Amid the pantomime of hate, the noble story of Terry and Otello breaking bread slipped between the cracks.

While the topic of Juventus and the trip to Turin was absorbing so much light, it was easy to forget that Liverpool still had Premier League duties to deal with before setting off for Italy, with a Saturday afternoon trip to Manchester City, and it was back to the unpredictability of domestic disputes as Benítez's side slumped to a 1-0 defeat, conceding the only goal in injury time to a spectacular volley by Kiki Musampa from the edge of the penalty area.

Neither team had been particularly impressive, and despite the nature of Musampa's finish there was a carelessness to the loss, with the goal ultimately stemming from a Liverpool throw-in, one point in the palm of their hand that would have been enough for them to, at least temporarily, leapfrog Everton into fourth place, and as if the trauma of shipping a late winner wasn't bad enough, Gerrard picking up a groin strain during the final minutes had already been a massive blow.

All Benítez and his team could do was attempt to shake off the double disappointment and refocus on Juventus, with, at least to those looking in from the outside, Champions League qualification now looking more likely to be obtained by winning the competition rather than claiming a top-four spot in the Premier League; by the Monday afternoon, confirmation had come that Gerrard would not be part of the travelling squad, which at least meant Benítez could plan without the illusion that his captain could still be available.

At this point, despite the defeat at Manchester City, the Liverpool players were still of the mind that qualifying through the Premier League was the most realistic route into the 2005/06 Champions League. Carragher later admitted to doubts about their chances of reaching and winning in Istanbul as the trip to Turin loomed, 'We didn't believe we could win the Champions League. The time we thought we could win it was when the final whistle went against Juventus.'

Pragmatism had been at play when it came to thinking ahead for Carragher, 'I always remember Stevie Gerrard, as he did most seasons, had the odd hamstring problem. That season, if we didn't qualify for the Champions League, I always thought there was a good chance Stevie would move on. We were battling with Everton; I always remember Stevie saying, "I'm not sure about my hamstring for Juventus away, what do you think?" My advice to him was, "Leave it, don't risk it." I said, "If you pull your hamstring, you'll be out for the rest of the season. We won't catch Everton and you're probably gone if we don't get the top four." I was thinking more of the future of Liverpool, Stevie staying at the club.'

Gerrard was now one of nine first-team players unavailable for selection to Benítez, and while the names of Alonso and Cissé were very welcome sights in the squad as it set off for Turin, there was a lot of relative inexperience on the flight too with Le Tallec and Warnock also joined by Darren Potter and John Welsh, all four with a significant chance of being involved in the game.

Before the football could take place, there was to be another round of diplomacy between Liverpool and Juventus, with chairman David Moores, his chief executive Rick Parry, along with Phil Neal and Ian Rush, flying out to Turin a day before Benítez and his players in order to take part in civic memorials and events, Parry taking time out to publicly urge for caution and respect from the projected 3,000 travelling Liverpool fans. The message was clear, and it asked for everyone to stay safe, to blend into the wallpaper, and to stick to official means of travel.

Playing their political parts with aplomb, Moores, Neal, and Rush did most of the handshakes and kissing of babies, with the trio travelling to Juventus's city centre headquarters to hand over the 'Memory and Friendship' banner that had been displayed at Anfield a week earlier. As black and white as the stripes on their shirts, while a cold shoulder and a clenched fist was the order of the day for some Juventus supporters, for others there was an appetite for accepting the olive branch that had been extended, with the sports journalist and Juve fan Paolo Franchetti penning an article in the *Daily Telegraph* on the morning of the game, citing a will from many of his fellow fans of the club to move on, and while nothing could be forgotten, there was very much a need for a fresh start.

Franchetti went on to quote another Juventus supporter, Marco Voltri, who had been at Heysel, 'I didn't speak for over a week for the shock of that night, but very much because of this I am aware of the importance of making a new start, to shake hands with Liverpool fans. If some Juventus fans don't understand this, it's their problem. I won't forget that night, but that doesn't mean we can't make a new start. We can and must do so.'

Marco's words cut through the pantomime better than most, with a rich articulateness and a point of view that goes to prove that football tribalism shouldn't come without terms and conditions. Sometimes the likeminded soul is watching the game at the other end of the stadium, while the intolerant voice that bellows out prejudice a row or two behind you, with the same-coloured scarf as the one you are wearing, is the real problem.

Volatility was inevitably surrounding the return game, however, with Juventus message boards awash with threats of reprisals, at a time when the domestic Italian game in general was suffering a huge spike in violent disorder, with the weekend prior to the visit of Liverpool to the Stadio Delle Alpi being marred by nationwide clashes across a variety of outposts, inclusive of Cava dei Tirreni, Palermo, Perugia, Rome, and Udine.

It had all made for a collective uprising that had injured 85 police officers and left a swathe of destruction in its wake, events that prompted Italy's interior minister, Giuseppe Pisanu, to threaten sanctions and stadium closures, the political and footballing authorities becoming increasingly desperate that the sport cleaned up its image ahead of the nation's ultimately unsuccessful bid to win the hosting rights from UEFA for the 2012 European Championship finals, a decision on which was just two years away.

Adding a further layer of unease to the backdrop of the occasion, 24 hours earlier the second leg of the Derby della Madonnina quarter-final between Internazionale and Milan had been abandoned with 20 minutes remaining after Milan goalkeeper Dida had been struck on the shoulder by a flare, one of many that would be lobbed into his team's penalty area from the Curva Nord, after the flashpoint of the contentious disallowing of a goal by Inter's Esteban Cambiasso.

Trailing 1-0 on the night and 3-0 on aggregate, even had Cambiasso's goal stood, Inter would have needed a further three goals to progress to the semi-finals, and the driving force of the disruptions clearly rested within a will to taint Milan's achievement in knocking their bitter rivals out of Europe's biggest competition rather than it being an impassioned protest of being dispossessed of a momentum-shifting pivot point in the tie.

Markus Merk, the referee at the San Siro, had made every attempt to restart the game, but again had to curtail matters within a minute of the resumption as more flares began to rain down on the Milan penalty area in yet another blow to the Federazione Italiana Giuoco Calcio and their hopes of the projection of a positive image to the rest of the world; this had been the second Champions League game on Italian soil during 2004/05 to fail to reach its natural completion, after the group stage encounter between Roma and Dynamo Kyiv was brought to an early end at the Stadio Olimpico when the referee that night, Anders Frisk, was struck by a coin.

A temporary prohibition in place, Turin became a city cast within a ring of steel in the days leading up to the second leg, with no possibility of a repeat of Köln where Benítez had stumbled into a bar full of Liverpool supporters on the eve of the game.

Four days prior to the arrival of Liverpool, Juventus had been at the Stadio Artemio Franchi to face the age-old festering animosity of Fiorentina, where a 3-3 draw was shared in a fixture that caused trouble to break out in Florence and Turin. In such circumstances, it was as if Liverpool and their supporters had arrived within a souvenir snow globe of a city which had already been violently shaken the previous weekend, with blood pressures into overdrive long before the first flight from

Merseyside had touched down on the runway at Turin-Caselle Airport.

Upon arrival in Turin, Liverpool fans were met by a leaflet of dos and don'ts, advisories that included not travelling to the city's suburbs, staying in groups at all times, and keeping scarves and banners under wraps until they were safely within the stadium. Those arriving on the day of the game were herded on to buses and transported straight to the Stadio Delle Alpi, while those who had flown into Milan and Genoa, with plans to drive onward to Turin, were headed off at makeshift checkpoints at motorway exits in order to be escorted to their destination. Some 1,000 police officers were deployed and split between the city centre and the stadium, two-thirds more than would usually be on duty for a Juventus Champions League tie.

Happily, the rain fell heavily on the eve of the match, and Turin's city centre was a relatively peaceful if somewhat eerie place 24 hours prior to kick-off, with no overt sightings of either visiting Liverpool supporters or platoons of brooding ultras, yet it was a stereotypical case of the calm before the storm as the day of the game brought a wave of violent intent as focus switched to the stadium.

Visiting supporters were brought through the turnstiles via a human tunnel of police protection, clouds of teargas being dispatched towards the local insurgents, who were trying to breach the thick blue line to reach the Liverpool fans as they arrived. Rather than focus on sanctioning individuals for acts of provocation and malice, the only sensible tactic was to stifle the possibility of direct confrontation. For their professionalism and skill, a police car was set alight, while helicopters constantly circled this epicentre of rancour. All the while the implemented prohibition was openly defied by vendors, who were selling cans and bottles of beer on the streets.

Having navigated the teargas outside, there was venom in the air within the Stadio Delle Alpi, and with the away section significantly isolated it needed a concerted effort for the Juventus supporters to reach their prey, be that with projectiles or in person. In the build-up to kick-off, over towards the visiting fans flew bottles, coins, and ripped-up plastic seats, among other projectiles, many of which were lobbed back in the directions from which they arrived. Occasionally, a determined soul would try to make a break across the terraced no man's land toward the visitors, with hard-hatted stewards grabbing hold of them and throwing them back among the home sections, while the assembled riot police watched on with a relative disinterest.

More teargas was even administered on the concourses of the home sections, with Juventus supporters exploring the scope to breach the away section from within the inner circle of the stadium, and all around this concrete bowl there was no repeat of the type of banners of friendship and reconciliation that were on display at Anfield, with Juventus banners running the gamut of the provocative, the insightful, the humorous, and the chilling, with slogans instead proclaiming messages such as 'Reds. Animals! English Shite', 'Easy to Speak,

Difficult to Pardon: Murderers', 'You Are More Ugly Than Camilla', and '15-4-89. Sheffield. God Exists' being some of the standout efforts.

Gloves off as far as some were concerned in the away section, in an article for *The Times*, Tony Evans made reference to two Liverpool supporters down at the front, hanging over the railings making abhorrent pushing and floppy arm gestures. It made for an unedifying situation, and exactly the type of smouldering box of fireworks that many of those who had lost loved ones at Heysel hadn't wanted to see unfold.

On the morning of the game, Andrea Lorentini, the 22-year-old grandson of Otello, and the son of Roberto, the doctor who had died in Section Z on those crumbling Brussels terraces 20 years earlier, had written in the pages of *La Stampa* that despite his up close and personal experience of the devastation that violence can cause, it was his will that hatred be left behind that evening. It was unfortunately to be an intelligence of thought that largely fell on deaf ears, however. Volatility prevailed.

Almost as if an afterthought, there was something entirely fitting to the occasion that the football itself meandered its way to a goalless draw, a result that was good enough to take Liverpool into the semi-finals ahead of their more highly regarded opponents, prompting a barrage of flares and fireworks being aimed with precision into the Stadio Delle Alpi's away section at Juventus's celebrating foe.

Without the services of Gerrard, Benítez turned to the returning Alonso to be the pivot around which the rest of Liverpool's players revolved, while Dudek got the nod in goal ahead of Carson. Hyypiä returned alongside the excellent Carragher in central defence once again, and Antonio Núñez was drafted in on to play nominally on the right of midfield, although tucked in to allow García play in behind Baroš. On the bench sat the figure of Djibril Cissé, set to complete his astonishing return to action just six months on from the double leg fracture that was close to ending his career.

A performance that was built upon discipline and resilience, nobody epitomised Liverpool's determination better than Carragher, who was utterly unbreakable in front of Dudek, who in turn was rarely at peril throughout a game in which Juventus were surprisingly ineffective in attack. With Alonso seeing all the angles, Biščan in perpetual motion alongside him, and García tireless in dropping off, through the perceived vulnerabilities of Liverpool appeared a spine that was strong yet flexible, and Capello simply couldn't spin a plan to pick it apart.

Del Piero subdued, Nedvěd blotted out, Ibrahimović often isolated, and Trezeguet absent, much of Capello's initial approach depended upon the talented but unpredictable Rubén Olivera's creativity, only for him to be replaced after the interval by his Uruguayan international team-mate Marcelo Zalayeta in a switch that made little difference to the home side's efforts during the second half, Juventus largely reduced to floating long balls into the Liverpool penalty area which were comfortably dealt with by Carragher and Hyypiä.

So untroubled were Liverpool on the pitch that when Cannavaro came as close as Juventus had all night 14 minutes from time, it was totally out of rhythm with the rest of their performance, with a Dudek save from an Emerson header just beyond the hour proving to be the only other threatening moment of note, Ibrahimović having been wasteful when well-placed during the early exchanges and lofting his shot harmlessly over the crossbar.

At the other end, restricting themselves to occasional counterattacks, Baroš could have given Liverpool some valuable breathing space early in the second half when sent clean through on Buffon only to direct his shot wide, and the sight of Cissé for the last 15 minutes, sent on to stretch the minds as well as the legs of the Juventus defence, was the cherry on the cake for Benítez on an evening when Liverpool's domination of midfield was the ultimate key to success.

Tellingly, Benítez had opted for a switch in formation, deploying Traoré as a third central defender rather than at left-back, with Finnan and Riise operating as wing-backs, dropping in as a back five when pressed and flooding the midfield whenever they were able to push Juventus back, not that Capello's side were overly advanced for any prolonged period of the game. Tactically, it gave Juventus's attacking players little space in central areas in which to work the ball into the channels, leaving them unable to play to the strengths of Ibrahimović. In essence, it was a masterclass of a setup by Benítez, with his players carrying out his plan to the letter.

Liverpool's progression to the semi-finals was fully deserved across the two legs, and in his post-match interviews Capello was quick to praise the industry of the visitors, cursing the lack of room in midfield as the key to his team's undoing. To prove how strong a team Benítez and his players had overcome, Juventus would go on to claim the Serie A title, finishing seven points clear of Carlo Ancelotti's Milan, a glory that they were later stripped of as part of the *Calciopoli* scandal.

Back in west London, José Mourinho would undoubtedly have been a studious observer of events at the Stadio Delle Alpi. Chelsea's success the previous evening against Bayern Munich now meant that a first all-English Champions League semi-final was looming. Once again, the odds would be stacked against Liverpool going any further in the competition. The odds don't always reflect the outcome, however.

Chapter Twelve

There's a Ghost in My House

JOY UNCONFINED at a job well done in Turin and the obtaining of a place in the semi-finals of the Champions League, it was now back to the monotonous slog of Premier League duties for a Liverpool side that found themselves four points adrift of fourth-placed Everton with only six fixtures left to play.

Having worked their way back to within one point of David Moyes's side after the win at home to Bolton Wanderers – although Everton were still marginally in the driving seat for Champions League qualification as Liverpool made the trip down the East Lancashire Road to face Stuart Pearce's Manchester City – it seemed that Rafael Benítez's side were all set to grab hold of the steering wheel down the final straight.

Defeat at the Etihad was a blow that was intensified 24 hours later by Everton's convincing victory at home to Crystal Palace, and now Liverpool were faced with a must-win game at Anfield against Tottenham Hotspur on a day when the blue half of Merseyside were handed a day off, as they had been due a trip to Highbury to face an Arsenal side that were instead involved in the FA Cup semi-finals. Here was the opportunity for Benítez and his team to close back to within one point of Everton, albeit with having played one game more than their neighbours.

Starkly, after positioning themselves on the shoulder of Everton with 21 points left to play for, Liverpool would go on to win only two of their remaining seven Premier League games, with one of those being on the final day at home to Aston Villa when no longer able to claim fourth place, collecting just eight points in the run-in. Across the same span of games, Moyes's team were only two points better off, gathering ten and even contriving to win only one of their last five fixtures, losing three times, although the last two of those defeats did come after they had secured Champions League qualification and their penultimate match was a 7-0 drubbing in their rearranged visit to Arsenal.

It was a damning indictment of Liverpool's Premier League difficulties that they weren't capable of putting adequate pressure on Everton across those last seven league games, beyond winning the Merseyside derby at Anfield; the fixtures between the second leg of the Champions League quarter-final against Juventus and the first leg of the semi-final against Chelsea were the perfect embodiment of their domestic inconsistencies of the 2004/05 season.

Tottenham, Portsmouth, and Crystal Palace, one step to the side, one forward, and one backwards; a draw at Anfield against Martin Jol's side, a win away versus Alain Perrin's outfit at Fratton Park, and a loss at Selhurst Park at the hands of Iain Dowie's relegation-bound team were a trio of games where even this inconsistent vintage of Liverpool should have been able to take at least seven points.

When Tottenham rolled into Anfield in mid-April, they hadn't won on their Premier League travels since Boxing Day, drawing two and losing four of their last six away days and mustering only two goals across 540 minutes of league football away from White Hart Lane. Another team that would limp sorrily across the season's finish line, Tottenham shouldn't have posed an issue for a Liverpool side with a Champions League semi-final to look forward to and fourth place still a possibility.

Falling behind to a stunning 40-yard strike from Erik Edman in the 12th minute, a shot that dipped dramatically after it cleared the head of a bewildered Jerzy Dudek, Liverpool were back on level terms just before the interval when Luis García sent a beauty of his own curling past Paul Robinson to end a fascinating but not scintillating first half in which the clash of differing formations had made for confusion for both teams at times.

With Jol setting up Tottenham in a 3-4-3 formation, Benítez had elected to go with the same pattern that he had fielded in Turin, with three central defenders of his own behind five across the midfield, Mauricio Pellegrino having returned to replace Djimi Traoré, Stephen Warnock being given a run out in place of John Arne Riise, and Steven Gerrard back from injury to dislodge Igor Biščan.

After 18 months of regression on the pitch, a sombre Gérard Houllier arrives at Anfield for the press conference to announce his departure from Liverpool Football Club, after five years in which he delivered a cup treble in 2000/01, along with further successes, a span of time in which he almost lost his life after suffering a dissected aorta.

All smiles for Houllier and Rick Parry after the announcement however, as they take to the pitch for some final photos. Along with the trophies he won, the outgoing Liverpool manager had modernised the club's structure and brought an end to the last remnants of the Spice Boys era. Unfortunately, the ill health Houllier had suffered had derailed the momentum of his reign.

In September 2002, Houllier's Liverpool were humbled by Rafael Benítez's Valencia, at the Mestalla, in the group stages of the Champions League. A difficult night for the visitors, in more ways than one, there was a lesson to be absorbed on the pitch, there was racism in the air, and Liverpool finished the game with ten men.

Just over a week beyond the 2004 UEFA Cup Final, an emotional Benítez announces his resignation from Valencia. Within his three years at the Mestalla, he had delivered European glory and two league titles, thus overturning the club's reputation as Spanish football's great underachievers. Frustrations over player recruitment primarily led to his exit.

A fortnight beyond walking away from Valencia, Benítez is finally unveiled as the new Liverpool manager, in succession to Houllier. It's straight down to work for the new man in the hotseat, as he heads off to Portugal to introduce himself to the players he has inherited, who are involved in the 2004 European Championship finals.

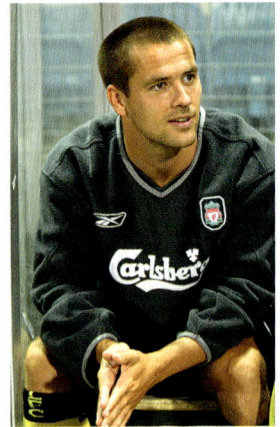

Throughout the summer of 2004, the departure from Anfield of Steven Gerrard had seemed a far more likely scenario, than that of Michael Owen. Yet, by the time of Liverpool's trip to face AK Graz in the third qualifying round of the Champions League, it was the other way around. Owen struck an awkward image on the bench, as his move to Real Madrid loomed.

Danny Murphy's sale comes as a bit of a surprise, but the arrival of Real Sociedad's Xabi Alonso is quite the coup. The cultured Basque is given quite the rustic baptism, in a defeat at Sam Allardyce's Bolton Wanderers. Here, Kevin Nolan introduces himself.

Along with Alonso, Luis García also strengthened Benítez's Iberian contingent, when signed from Barcelona. Player and manager had linked before, at CD Tenerife, and the explosively skilful attacker would make a cult hero of himself, after a magical home debut at Anfield, against West Bromwich Albion.

It's a winning start in Group A for Liverpool, with a commanding performance against Monaco. On an evening when Benítez's side created chances aplenty, it was left to Milan Baroš to net a late goal to secure a 2-0 victory. Didier Deschamps' much-altered team had contested the 2004 Champions League Final.

Without the injured Gerrard, who was recovering from a broken metatarsal, it's a frustrating evening in Athens, against Olympiacos. Ieroklis Stoltidis rises above the Liverpool defence to head home the only goal of the game. Despite the late red card for Anastasios Pantos, the visitors fail to take advantage.

On an astonishing night at Anfield, Liverpool score three times in the second half, at home to Olympiacos, to claim their passage into the knockout stages, having trailed to a Rivaldo free kick at the interval. Florent Sinama-Pongolle and Neil Mellor have been the unlikely heroes, prior to Gerrard flashing home the clincher, with only four minutes remaining.

Dietmar Hamann celebrates, having grabbed Liverpool's third goal, during the first leg of their last-16 clash with Bayer Leverkusen, at Anfield. Moments later, a Jerzy Dudek error gives the Bundesliga outfit a glimmer of hope for the second leg, although it doesn't detract from a job well done.

Any concerns about the late away goal conceded in the first leg are blown away at the Bay Arena, in emphatic fashion. García scores twice, and is denied a hat-trick, as a place in the quarter-finals is secured with style and substance.

Amicizia. Friendship is offered, but the reactions are mixed. When Liverpool and Juventus faced one another for the first time since the Heysel disaster, an extensive programme of events were organised ahead of the first leg at Anfield, and while the olive branch was accepted by some Italian visitors, other understandably remained defiant.

García is the Champions League talisman once again for Liverpool, as he nets a spectacular goal to make it 2-0 against a shell-shocked Juventus.

Alonso makes his return to action in Turin, while Gerrard is absent with a hamstring injury. A consummate performance sees Liverpool into the semi-finals, on a volatile evening off the pitch. Juventus supporters make their feelings about their visitors known.

García wheels away in celebration, as he snatches the only goal of the semi-final second leg, and Anfield erupts. One of the most electric nights that the old stadium has ever experienced, the arguments of whether the ball crossed the line or not still rage on to this day. Over 180 minutes, plus injury time, Liverpool were deserved winners.

On the cusp of half-time at the Atatürk Olympic Stadium, Hernan Crespo, on loan with Milan from Chelsea, makes it 3-0 to Carlo Ancelotti's side. Surely the 2005 Champions League Final is over?

One goal back, and a foot in the door. Gerrard implores his team-mates and supporters alike to raise their game and believe. Anything is possible.

Dida with the save, but Alonso is first to the rebound, as Liverpool make it 3-3. With the scoreline now level, there can only be one winner from here …

Five-and-a-half minutes of madness. Liverpool have stunned the Milan fans into disbelief.

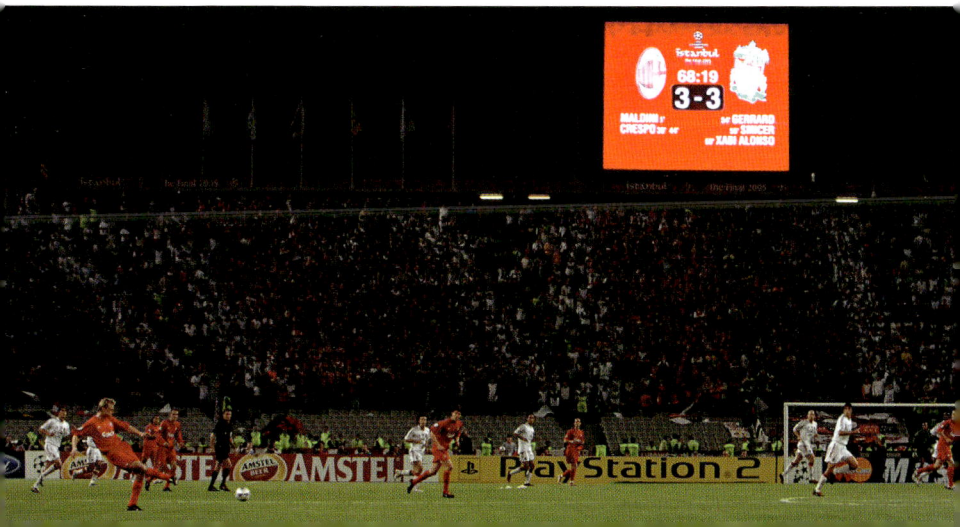

Jerzy Dudek makes his remarkable double save from Andriy Shevchenko, deep into extra time. Milan's hopes are arguably fatally shattered within this moment. Liverpool's Polish goalkeeper will soon be replaced by Benítez, but his place in Anfield folklore is obtained.

Sealed with a kiss. Jamie Carragher watches on as Gerrard puckers up with the trophy. Carragher's determined and consistent defending had been a key element of Liverpool's 2004/05 Champions League success. His presence was invaluable and Benítez's decision to restore him to a central defensive role was as crucial as the retention of Gerrard and signing of Alonso.

A riot of red. Old Big Ears is back in Liverpool hands, as Gerrard follows in the footsteps of Emlyn Hughes, Phil Thompson and Graeme Souness in being a European Cup-winning Liverpool captain. The impossible dream has been realised.

A heroes' homecoming. St George's Hall, on Lime Street, marks the culmination of the Liverpool parade. Many of the supporters who were present in Istanbul hadn't even made it back yet, but this was the chance for the entire city to turn out in celebration.

For Liverpool, with the extra man in midfield, it meant that Xabi Alonso was able to spin his magic for much of the afternoon, and the second half became the footballing equivalent of an Ealing Studios farce with genius and madness being evident in equal measure. Fast out of the blocks upon the resumption, the otherwise anonymous Fernando Morientes, who had returned as the replacement for the still domestically suspended Milan Baroš, forced Robinson into an excellent reflex save only for the home side to ludicrously concede a second Tottenham goal a short few minutes later.

With Liverpool's luck emphatically out once again, incredulously a Robbie Keane header found its way past a stranded Dudek after a Frédéric Kanouté cross and via a deflection off Jamie Carragher, and when just moments later Gerrard sent a penalty high and wide into the Kop, it felt like the footballing Gods had come to Anfield to collect their taxes for overseeing smooth Champions League progression.

Five minutes beyond Gerrard's miss from 12 yards, Sami Hyypiä was on target with a sumptuous volley to square the scoreline once again, but try as they might a winning goal simply would not materialise, with García, Steve Finnan, and Morientes all squandering great opportunities, and Gerrard even hitting the post in the closing stages. In a game in which Liverpool had enjoyed 71 per cent of the possession it was very much a case of two points dropped, and with El Hadji Diouf scoring Bolton's winning goal away at Charlton Athletic, Sam Allardyce's side had collected three points at The

Valley that were enough to lift them above Benítez and his players and into fifth place.

Now three points behind Everton, who also held a game in hand, this was the weekend where chat began to surround the potential concept of Moyes's side perhaps not qualifying for the Champions League after all, even if they were to finish fourth, should Liverpool go on to Istanbul to lift 'Old Big Ears' for the fifth time in their history, from outside the top four of the Premier League. It was a hot topic of conversation but not entirely without ambiguities.

Article 1.03 of UEFA's regulations was clear in its directions that it was up to each individual national football association to request any potential amendment to its list of qualifying teams for the Champions League and UEFA Cup, meaning that there was no automatic provision for the reigning champions of Europe to have the right to defend their crown.

Essentially, UEFA fully expected that any self-respecting association would absolutely want a Champions League-winning team of theirs to be back in the competition the following season as the holders. Precedent of such an occurrence had even been recent, as when Real Madrid won the Champions League in 1999/2000 they did so without finishing in the top four in Spain, which meant that Real Zaragoza, despite finishing fourth that season, were instead placed in the UEFA Cup by the Liga Nacional de Fútbol Profesional. Of course, the English would predictably go their own way on such matters, with a messy summer unwittingly ahead.

At a distance of five weeks still to be traversed before the Champions League Final, the concept of Liverpool making such a diplomatic argument a reality seemed a moot point to most independent observers with Chelsea widely expected to progress to Istanbul, and even then, should Benítez's side somehow pull a surprise and reach the final, Milan would surely be waiting to dismantle them.

Four days beyond the disappointment of dropping two points at home to Tottenham, Liverpool were faced with a midweek trip to Fratton Park to go up against a mildly rejuvenated Portsmouth, a club that had indulged in a season of dysfunction of their own and were now on their third manager of a campaign of attrition.

Having parted ways with Harry Redknapp towards the end of November, owner Milan Mandarić had turned to his Croatian compatriot Velimir Zajec, who had arrived as executive director much to Redknapp's visible unease earlier in the year, and after a promising caretaker span in charge he was appointed to the role on a more permanent footing shortly before Christmas only for the wheels to dramatically fall off after the turn of the year.

Picking up just one win from his last 12 league games at the helm, in early April Mandarić opted to rehouse Zajec to his original role in order to bring in the former Olympique de Marseille head coach Alain Perrin, who then took four from his first six possible points with an entertaining victory at home to Charlton and a hard-fought draw at Birmingham City, which meant that

Liverpool were walking into an arena where there was a degree of new manager bounce at play.

Persevering with three central defenders, Pellegrino dropped down to the bench to be replaced by Traoré, while Warnock was absent after he departed the pitch injured in the first half against Tottenham. Added to this, Gerrard also found himself among the substitutes in the name of Benítez protecting him ahead of the Champions League semi-final games, while Antonio Núñez dropped out entirely, which all combined to bring Riise back in from the start along with Bišćan and Baroš.

As a sign of the injury problems Liverpool had had to contend with all season, the return of the Czech Republic striker marked the first time that Benítez had been able to call upon the complete trio of Baroš, Djibril Cissé, and Morientes for any one given game since the former Real Madrid man's arrival, and it was the Spanish international who opened the scoring after just four minutes, prodding home his own rebound from close range as the ball bounced back off Jamie Ashdown after his initial effort at goal.

In an eventful start Portsmouth had had a goal of their own disallowed with only 41 seconds on the clock, Lomana LuaLua falling foul of the linesman's flag, and it was a swift turnaround from such a potentially poor start for Liverpool when Morientes made it 1-0, laid in by Riise after smart work by Baroš.

Increasingly frustrated by Liverpool's highly effective offside trap, when Portsmouth did grab their 33rd-minute equaliser it was totally against the run of play, Diomansy

Kamara putting away the rebound this time after Finnan had made a goal-line clearance from Arjan de Zeeuw's initial header following a Matthew Taylor corner, only for the visitors to regain the lead just before half-time, García profiting from a fine cross from the right by Finnan.

It was to be the last contribution to the game by García, who Benítez withdrew at the interval in another act of self-protection ahead of the engagements to come against Chelsea, a switch that gave Vladimír Šmicer a valuable 45 minutes during a largely uneventful second half in which chances were sparse, and Gerrard got to stretch his legs for the last 20 minutes or so in place of Bišćan, with a further 15 minutes as part of Cissé's carefully managed return to action.

These were three crucial points for Liverpool but they were nullified by news of Everton's narrow victory at home to a Manchester United side who ended the evening with nine men after the dismissals of Gary Neville and Paul Scholes in an ill-tempered game, although on the up side it had been a win on the south coast for the Reds that was good enough to lift Benítez's men back up into fifth, ahead of Bolton, who had been held to a draw 24 hours earlier at home to relegation-threatened Southampton.

Three days beyond their victory at Fratton Park, Liverpool headed to Selhurst Park to take on a Crystal Palace side that had failed to pick up a win in their previous six league games, had won only six times all season, and were off the foot of the table on goal difference alone having succumbed to an insipid midweek defeat at Ewood Park against Blackburn Rovers.

On an afternoon when Benítez's team took to the pitch in possession of the knowledge that a win would put them level on points with Everton after the Blues had dropped two at home to Birmingham City in the early kick-off, it was with a startling lack of drive that Liverpool drifted to their tenth league reversal on the road of 2004/05, undone when Andrew Johnson scored the only goal of the game, instinctively diverting a glancing header past Dudek, teed up not by a cross but instead Wayne Routledge's slashed volley that was all set to go comfortably wide.

With 11 minutes of the first half still to play, and the entirety of the second half to remedy their situation, rather than seek momentum Liverpool instead meandered through the remainder of the match, as Alyson Rudd in *The Times* put it, 'Like a chap in debt who maintains a carefree air because he has a lottery ticket in his pocket,' events that were not lost on Carragher in his post-match opinions, 'We know we've got a massive game coming up on Wednesday but this was a massive game as well. It is particularly galling because we knew the Everton score before the game, and we were all speaking about that. But every time they don't take maximum points, and we know we've got to capitalise, we don't do it.'

Lodged within a crevice where the first leg of the Champions League semi-final loomed on one side and lingering hopes of a top-four finish in the Premier League refused to melt away on the other, Benítez had made four changes to the starting line-up that had won at Portsmouth with Alonso and García rested entirely, while

Riise and Bišćan dropped down to the bench, ushering back Gerrard, along with Pellegrino, John Welsh, and Anthony Le Tallec, the manager again opting for three central defenders, at least until the once again struggling Pellegrino was replaced by Riise early in the second half.

On a frustrating afternoon, Benítez had already been forced to make a first-half change when sending on Darren Potter in place of the injured Baroš, who was unwisely allowed to labour on for another 36 minutes after absorbing an uncompromising challenge within 60 seconds of the start from Tony Popovic, sustaining a knee wound that eventually required four stitches, while even the introduction of Cissé midway through the second half failed to turn the tide of the game for the visitors. When Gerrard extended Gábor Király into a late save at full stretch, it was Liverpool's only significant effort at goal.

Apart from the extra legwork afforded to Cissé, there were very few positives that Benítez could take from the defeat and it was a highly subdued visiting section that made their way to the Selhurst Park exit gates on a day when, for Chelsea, it had been a very different experience over in west London with their defeat of Fulham at Stamford Bridge moving them to within one win of clinching the Premier League title.

Continuing domestic difficulties aside, Benítez could at least take solace in the quiet confidence that some of his players were viewing the trip to Chelsea for the first leg of the semi-final, with Alonso being front and centre of the positivity when sent out to be a voice of reason 48 hours prior to the game. In Paul Walker's article for *The Independent* the day before the first leg, the cultured Spanish international midfielder pointed out that the natural reaction to knocking out Juventus was the burgeoning confidence that, in the Champions League at least, Liverpool could beat anyone.

Alonso was also intelligent enough not to be drawn into talk of vengeance over the broken ankle he had sustained from Frank Lampard the last time he had faced Chelsea, instead playing down his impending resumption of midfield hostilities with the England international. Alonso was quoted in the same article in terms of how he had spoken several times with Lampard since the incident, and that the former West Ham United man had been the one to approach him with an unreserved apology within the days following the injury.

Expertly drawing the sting of the situation, Alonso's measured opinions deflected the focus further on to Chelsea and away from Liverpool in the build-up, and whether sincere or not, José Mourinho opted for an attempt to kill his opposition with kindness, declaring in his own press conference that it was no surprise to him that Liverpool had reached the semi-finals, his only astonishment being that Benítez's side had not been able to prosper in the Premier League. In fact, rather than inflammatory, Mourinho was loosely lavish in his praise of a counterpart he deemed to be one of the best managers in football, at the helm of a club that was respected all around the world.

At Stamford Bridge, the Liverpool line-up largely selected itself, certainly once Baroš was passed fit to play, with Pellegrino and Morientes dropping out of European combat once again due to being cup-tied; added to this, Le Tallec was stood down to a place among the substitutes and Welsh was sidelined completely as Riise, Bišćan, and García returned along with Alonso, with the inclusion of Bišćan particularly speaking of a defiantly stereotypical first-leg away approach to the tie by Benítez and his team, rather than them yielding to the temptation to deal with the evening as if it were a Premier League fixture.

Mourinho clearly expected such a scenario and had even been considered enough to assure his players and the Chelsea supporters that a 0-0 draw at Stamford Bridge would not be a calamity given that his team had already won at Anfield that season, confident in their abilities as he was that they could do so again. Within this, the conundrum over which version of Liverpool would arrive in west London was obviously playing on the Portuguese's mind. It was almost as if he was psyching himself out, doing a significant amount of Benítez's work for him.

While Benítez's side slotted into place without fuss or conjecture, Mourinho had much to ponder, with Damian Duff looking increasingly unlikely to be fit enough to play and Arjen Robben only just having returned from injury almost three months on from his last start in a Chelsea shirt. It would come as a surprise to all to see Tiago deployed on the left-hand side of the Chelsea attack in what seemed at the time to be a choice that lacked Mourinho's early years trademark bravado at Stamford Bridge.

In part due to Liverpool's meticulously organised approach to the game, in part due to Mourinho's overthinking, Chelsea played straight into the hands of Benítez and his team, the visitors reverting to the DNA of their European pedigree after the dysfunction of domestic matters at Selhurst Park four days earlier.

Weight of expectation resting heavily on them, it was an unexpectedly nervy start by Chelsea with Liverpool dominating the first ten minutes, Gerrard pressing higher up the pitch to supplement Baroš as the home side went into retreat, the lack of the outlet usually provided by Duff and Robben making it difficult for the home team to get a foothold in the game during the early exchanges, with those roles instead falling to Joe Cole and Eiður Guðjohnsen, the latter being deployed in a less familiar position on the left.

A first half of hastily snatched efforts, fine goalkeeping from Petr Čech, and acute profligacy meant that the game somehow reached the interval goalless, Lampard having wasted the best opportunity from six yards while Čech denied Riise and Baroš from obtaining an all-important away goal with crucial saves.

What followed was a second half that amounted to footballing shadow boxing, with neither side willing to risk rolling the dice if it were to have any danger of leading to conceding a goal themselves, matters eventually simmering down to a midfield stalemate and stranglehold defensive displays on an evening when Dudek didn't have a save of substance to make.

Try as he might, Mourinho simply could not work his way around the conundrum that Benítez had presented him with, even when throwing Robben into the fray for the final half an hour to replace the ineffectual Tiago, Finnan stifling the Dutchman with such an excellent blotting out job on the talented winger that Chelsea's most creative element became increasingly selfish whenever in possession of the ball, thus making a goal for the home side even more unlikely.

Beyond Čech's command of his penalty area, ably aided by the immaculate defending of Ricardo Carvalho, there was only really Claude Makélélé who came away from the game with credit for Chelsea, with John Terry occasionally overwhelmed by the occasion, Glen Johnson pinned in at right-back, William Gallas labouring out of position at left-back, and Didier Drogba having struggled with a lack of supply from Lampard, Cole, Tiago, and Guðjohnsen.

For Liverpool, it was another masterclass in defending with Carragher not putting a foot wrong, while Hyypiä made a series of critical interceptions and was dominant in the air, all of which was added to by Traoré cancelling out Cole, who along with Finnan collectively protected a largely untroubled but occasionally jittery Dudek.

In midfield, Gerrard had duelled with Makélélé throughout in an intriguing subplot, although the Liverpool captain's overall performance was vaguely subdued, a possible result of having undergone dental surgery on the morning of the game; added to this, Bišćan had revelled once more in undertaking the more thankless tasks, Alonso sprayed the passes around and oozed composure, while García and Riise were effective enough to keep Chelsea's full-backs too occupied to offer much of a threat going forwards, the five of them successfully flooding the centre ground, if for long periods leaving Baroš, and then for the last 25 minutes Cissé, a little too isolated.

A proficient job done, one in which Chelsea were reduced in the final stages to pragmatic long and easily dealt with balls into the penalty area, the only blot on the Liverpool copybook coming away from their evening's work being the harsh yellow card picked up by Alonso that would rule him out of the second leg. With the post-match chatter basically drifting into a tussle over who had secured the moral victory, Mourinho claimed that his team had obtained a very good result and that there would be more pressure on Liverpool in the return. Benítez, however, expressed his opinion that the visitors had controlled proceedings, and that while his team would need to win at Anfield there was every possibility that they would do so.

Away section bouncing at Stamford Bridge, it was certainly a jubilant set of Liverpool supporters who were eventually allowed to make their way to the exit gates, content in the knowledge of the cauldron they would create on home soil six days later and soothed by the thoughts that Chelsea had lost on their last three Champions League away days, at Porto, Barcelona, and Bayern Munich. Yes, there was still much work to be done if Liverpool were to make it to Istanbul, but there was nothing Mourinho could say to sugarcoat a disappointing first-leg outcome for the Premier League champions elect, the bare bones being that his team lacked creativity and didn't force Dudek into a save of significance.

Within the following day's glow, the cloud over the question of whether or not there would be a way back into the Champions League for Liverpool in 2005/06 grew a little darker with word emerging that such a fate for Benítez's team would rest in the hands of the Professional Game Board, a sub-committee offshoot of the main Football Association board, comprising a six-man deployment made up of David Dein, Phil Gartside, Peter Heard, Rupert Lowe, Dave Richards, and David Sheepshanks, upwardly mobile board members, past and present, of Arsenal, Bolton Wanderers, Colchester United, Southampton, Sheffield Wednesday, and Ipswich Town respectively, the vast majority of them being men who were set to be associated with clubs that would reside outside the Premier League in 2005/06.

Positive vibes going hand-in-hand with negative connotations for Liverpool, as the weekend rolled into view ambiguity surrounded the chances of Robben and Duff being involved at Anfield for the second leg, the Dutchman having limped away from the Stamford Bridge pitch at the end of the first leg after aggravating his left ankle once again while the Irishman's troublesome hamstring continued to cause Mourinho concern.

With the potential absences of Duff and Robben providing a boost to Liverpool's chances, rancour began to rise over the loss of Alonso, with Guðjohnsen coming under critical scrutiny over his part in the yellow card that was flashed by Alain Sars, the Icelandic international being irate enough to issue strenuous denials of stories that he had goaded the Spaniard over the suspension he would have to serve.

Maintaining Mourinho's post-match projection of bravado that the draw was a better result for Chelsea than it was for Liverpool, Čech and Cole were bullish enough to suggest that they were more than capable of going to Anfield to score and keep a clean sheet, and while there was merit in what they believed given that Chelsea had done just that in the Premier League four months earlier, they were also falling into the trap of viewing the encounter ahead as a domestic matter rather than the European tie it was instead.

In contrast, Benítez and his players would not be drawn into predictions and finger pointing. While Mourinho and his squad weren't backwards in coming forwards when it came to self-promotion, the Reds opted to keep their powder dry and their cards close to their chest. Their focus was, without doubt, intensely zeroed in on the second leg, but they would first need to deal with the distraction of a Premier League visit of Middlesbrough to Anfield on the Saturday afternoon, while Mourinho's side travelled to Bolton Wanderers for the later kick-off where they would be able to secure their first league title in 50 years.

Against Middlesbrough, Benítez made five changes to the line-up he had sent out at Stamford Bridge as Hyypiä and García dropped down to the bench, with

THERE'S A GHOST IN MY HOUSE

Traoré, Bišćan, and Baroš not involved at all in the 16 on duty, while back in came Pellegrino, Warnock, Núñez, Morientes and Harry Kewell, the Australian returning to the starting 11 for the first time since the League Cup Final defeat to Chelsea over two months earlier.

Benítez had reintroduced Kewell as a substitute for the final five minutes at Stamford Bridge and here was his big chance to impress over 90 minutes, yet he, but not he alone, failed to perform against a stubborn and well-organised Middlesbrough side, visitors whose determined defence was marshalled by a 34-year-old Gareth Southgate, who was sporting a headband under which resided the ten stitches that he had needed to knit together a head wound sustained three days earlier at Newcastle United after a gruesome collision with Alan Shearer.

While one veteran central defender excelled, another continued his struggles against the volatile variables of English football as Szilárd Németh bulldozed his way past Pellegrino with only four minutes on the clock before dispatching the ball past a badly exposed Dudek. The former Valencia man was not to reappear after the interval.

Pellegrino had been a peculiar conundrum. Widely reputed to be a valuable presence in the dressing room, on the pitch he had proved a repeated liability, with the Middlesbrough game marking his 11th appearance in the Premier League, of which he had been on the winning side only twice and on the losing side six times. Since his arrival in January he had sat out just three league games, all of them ending in a win.

Another two Premier League points dropped, Liverpool still had 38 minutes in which to conjure up a winning goal beyond Gerrard's stunning 25-yard screamer of an equaliser, yet it was to be a story of more frustration on an afternoon when Everton were beaten at Fulham, Benítez's side carelessly passing up on the opportunity to close the gap on their neighbours to just one point.

Conversely, for Chelsea, this had been the day on which they had finally clinched the Premier League title, doing so with three games to spare, although Mourinho had needed to give his players a piece of his mind and food for thought at half-time after an insipid first half at Bolton. For the second leg of the semi-final they would be arriving at Anfield as the newly crowned champions of England.

As the day of the second leg dawned, all considerations of domestic difficulties were shelved by Liverpool, however. Benítez's side had shown that they were more than at home in Europe and they would prove the point once again, with Gerrard in particular eager to be the master of destiny in a game where extra spice was stirred in with chatter that Mourinho was beginning to turn his attentions in potential summer midfield recruits away from the lad from Huyton.

Benítez, casting off his usual cloak of measured conservatism in the pre-match press conference, was confident and assertive about his team's hopes, defiantly stating that Chelsea would lose, as if he were a man who had seen the future long before a kick of the ball had been made. When it was pointed out that Chelsea's Champions League form had been good too, his reply came with straight bat steel and a smile that betrayed nothing. 'Until tomorrow,' he stated.

Despite showing no shortage of confidence in the outcome, Benítez then proceeded to paint a picture where Liverpool had nothing to lose, claiming that a win would make them heroes while defeat would be widely viewed as the expected result against what he billed as the most expensive team in the world, the champions of England, with a lot of admired players, and one of the best coaches in the game.

Confidence combined with deflection from Benítez, and up next was Mourinho, who attempted to turn the question of pressure around, decreeing that win or lose Chelsea would be welcomed back to Stamford Bridge on Saturday for the visit of Charlton as heroes for winning the Premier League title, whereas he doubted that Anfield would be quite as warm with their team should they miss out on a place in the final. Mourinho was also swift to downplay the factor of the atmosphere his players were about to face, claiming that the spotlight of expectation did not blind them, that he had experienced fantastic atmospheres many times before and that they would enjoy what Anfield had to offer. The trap was set.

Without the suspended Alonso, Benítez was able to call upon the returning Hamann, making for the only change from the line-up Liverpool had started with in the first leg, although tactically deploying two defensive midfielders this time with another Champions League start being handed to Bišćan, and Gerrard being fielded as the link between midfield and attack in behind Baroš.

With tickets changing hands for upwards of £1,200, for everyone who was able to click through the Anfield turnstiles or be in a position to flash their press passes to security, this was to be an evening that would sear the soul for ever one way or another, with the air crackling in anticipation in the hours leading up to the game.

Even before they reached Anfield, already Chelsea were being psyched out of their stride with Duff once again ruled out and Mourinho not willing to put Robben into his starting 11, thus restricting the expansion of his own midfield. Then the visitors' coach had to plot its way through the sea of red it was confronted by as it rolled slowly towards the stadium, faced as they were by the first clear indicator that they would not be experiencing the domestic atmosphere Liverpool's supporters usually provide them but instead the European drumbeat that even Alessandro Del Piero had been stunned by when Juventus came to town.

It took just four minutes for the decisive goal to materialise, and the rumble of contention has never abated ever since. Riise, cutting in from the left and evading the attentions of Carvalho, rolled the ball infield towards Gerrard, who watched it all the way yet also spotted the run of Baroš from the corner of his eye and then played the most outrageously sumptuous of dinked lobs with the outside of his right boot into the path of the onrushing Czech striker, who had now found himself in the Chelsea penalty area and bearing down on Čech.

In the blink of an eye Baroš was aware of the fast-closing Čech, and he attempted to hook the ball over his compatriot and into the Kop end net only to be clattered by the goalkeeper and sent sprawling to the turf, the ball now breaking to García, who with his left foot sent it onward toward goal, flicking off the desperate lunge of Terry and taking just enough pace off the shot to allow William Gallas the opportunity to clear.

Gallas indeed made contact with the ball and to him and his Chelsea team-mates the Frenchman had saved the day, except the roar of the Kop and the wheeling away in celebration of García offered an alternative outcome to the situation, as the Slovak referee Ľuboš Micheľ awarded a goal to Liverpool, with bedlam ensuing. As the vibrations took hold around Anfield the television cameras shook violently, Benítez appealed for calm heads, and Mourinho shrugged his bewilderment to his assistant Steve Clarke.

In the directors' box, legendary figures of the Reds' glorious past were as delirious as the fans, while Brian Barwick, the Liverpool-supporting chief executive of the Football Association, was a man caught between two stools, surely revelling in his beloved team rolling back the years while also mindful of the political football that would soon have an extra bounce to it, over the argument of a Champions League-winning Liverpool being prospectively denied the right to defend their crown.

For Chelsea, the crucial element of composure was lost, and while Liverpool would retreat into protection mode, always on the lookout to spring forth on the break, the plentiful periods of possession that the visitors were permitted made little difference to the ebb and flow of proceedings with Dudek not called upon to make a save until a 68th-minute Lampard free kick.

Increasingly animated on the touchline and desperate for a way back into the tie, Mourinho threw on Robben and Mateja Kežman in place of Cole and Tiago, the compact nature of the Chelsea starting line-up being easily subdued by Liverpool's watertight defence and the protection offered by Hamann and Bišćan, a blanket that was so effective that for the final 15 minutes Robert Huth was added to the picture as an emergency target man, Mourinho again reverting to high balls into the Liverpool penalty area just as he had done at Stamford Bridge in the first leg.

Frenetic and frantic in their efforts to procure an equaliser, Robben skied a shot into the Kop when well positioned, and when the board went up for six minutes of injury time it was the first time across the two games that a genuine nervousness set in for Liverpool as Chelsea pressed for a rabbit from the hat moment that would instead take them to Istanbul.

Of course, the moment almost came, as with only seconds remaining Guðjohnsen flashed 'that' shot across the face of Dudek's goal only for it to blissfully fly wide of the far post. Upon the final whistle the release of energy on the pitch and in the stands could have generated light and heat for miles around as the party got into full swing, and travel plans for the final began with immediate effect.

In his bid to counteract the feared Chelsea onslaught, Benítez had introduced Cissé in place of Baroš on the hour, and the man who almost never kicked a ball again was the recipient of Liverpool's best chance of extending their lead. While he wasn't able to take it, his speed was a constant headache for Terry, Carvalho, Geremi, and Gallas, while it was a bold move by the manager to opt Kewell in for the last 20 minutes in place of the tiring Hamann, and to throw on Núñez during the final minutes in a bid to run the ball into the corners when withdrawing García, the evening's ultimate hero.

Magnificent performances all round for Liverpool, but particularly by Carragher, Hyypiä, Finnan, Hamann, and Gerrard. There had been a heady mix of dependability, tenacity, desire, determination, and focus that had been missing so many times on a week-to-week basis in the Premier League, but here they were, kicking back, cracking open the beers, and able to put their feet up to watch the second leg of the other semi-final between PSV Eindhoven and Milan the following night.

Not one Liverpool player came out second-best in their respective duels, and while Mourinho would refuse to accept that García's goal had crossed the line, he was the height of magnanimity out on the pitch at the end, going around every Liverpool player to congratulate them and applauding the home supporters as he made his way towards the tunnel. Up in the directors' box, Roman Abramovich added his own applause to the outcome, as if accepting of the realism that money simply cannot buy everything, while the Chelsea players, to a man, were rendered stunned to disbelief as they soaked up the pain of defeat within the cauldron of a volcanic Anfield atmosphere, the visiting supporters held as an unwilling but entirely captive audience.

Within the slipstream of an incredible occasion, Gerrard declared it to have been the greatest night of his life, George Sephton, Liverpool's long-serving matchday announcer, thanked everyone in the stands for their contribution, deeming that he had never seen anything like it in all his years at the club, while Benítez and Carragher were quick to note that the job still needed to be completed. His message was that we were going to Istanbul to win.

Awestruck, many across the media were delighted and moved by Liverpool's act of defiance in overcoming the rouble-rich champions, sideswiped by the seething humanity that had been on show at Anfield, with Simon Barnes in *The Times* penning a piece that revelled in the havoc that had been at play on a night when the noise on the Kop hit a high of 119.8 decibels; the newspaper's chief sports writer proffered the opinion that it hadn't been García who had scored the winning goal at all, instead it had been prodded home via havoc, having been created by havoc, on a night when Liverpool prevailed due to the crowd inflicting their will on proceedings. In an ever-increasingly corporate product, this had been Liverpool reviving the lost art of footballing soul.

Chaos theory or not, the Reds had turned the season on its head, and there were just three weeks to wait until the pilgrimage to the Atatürk Olympic Stadium could begin.

Chapter Thirteen

The Miracle

ONWARD RUMBLED the row over whether or not the
ball crossed the line for the goal that had sent Liverpool
into the 2005 Champions League Final. Chelsea's beaten
manager and his players were unequivocal in their
opinions that it had very much not crossed the line,
as they directed most of their ire towards the Slovak
linesman, Roman Slyško, the man who had nodded his
approval for a goal.

What Chelsea's highly vocal representatives were a
little more circumspect on was the concept that the
alternative to a goal being awarded was a red card
being flashed at Petr Čech and a penalty being given
for his flattening of Milan Baroš, something that the
referee Ľuboš Micheľ had denoted would have been
the case had the goal not been deemed legitimate. In
effect, Luis García's goal was by far the better option
for Chelsea, with 86 minutes plus injury time still to
be played. Stamford Bridge anger really needed to be
channelled toward themselves, but there was clearly
no appetite there for taking a long, hard look in the
mirror.

A huge talking point all the same, analysis began to border on the ludicrous, with renewed calls for the introduction of goal-line technology while various experts argued the toss over whether García's shot had crossed the line or not. In an article in *The Independent*, Dr Mike Spann, a lecturer at Birmingham University's School of Electronic, Electrical and Computer Engineering, assessed a series of images to scientifically conclude it was indeed a goal, while a Sky Sports computerised re-enactment suggested it hadn't crossed the line. Meanwhile, ITV News commissioned Hawkeye to come to the same conclusion as Sky Sports' findings. Not that anyone within the Anfield bubble cared in the slightest.

Next up for Liverpool was the first of two Premier League games that sat ahead of the Champions League Final, and a trip to Highbury, where it had now become a win-or-bust situation with regards the now slim hopes of overhauling Everton for fourth place, after David Moyes's side had beaten Newcastle United at Goodison Park 24 hours earlier to leave the Reds six points adrift.

Aware of the last chance saloon element involved, Rafael Benítez made just one change to the starting line-up that had ridden into battle against Chelsea, with Xabi Alonso returning to the midfield in place of Igor Biščan. Within half an hour Arsenal were in possession of a 2-0 lead, and Everton were well on the way to securing fourth place, and at least provisional qualification for the 2005/06 Champions League.

Goals from Robert Pires and José Antonio Reyes, scored within three minutes of one another leading up to that 30-minute mark, put the game out of reach for Liverpool before it had really begun, and when married to a largely meek opening 45 minutes from the visitors it was only natural to fear the worst for the second half. Yet despite the forlorn situation in terms of the evaporation of any lingering prospect of a top-four finish, the introductions of Djibril Cissé and Harry Kewell in place of Baroš and John Arne Riise at the start of the second half made for a positive reaction, with Benítez tweaking his formation to allow Steven Gerrard to drop back into midfield from his more advanced position behind Baroš, with Kewell instead supporting Cissé higher up the pitch. Within six minutes of the restart the captain had dragged his team back to within one goal of Arsenal, picking the ball up from Dietmar Hamann's excellent lay-off before sending it arrowing past Jens Lehmann from distance via an added flick off the vibrant and dangerous Cesc Fàbregas.

For a brief spell Liverpool then looked the more likely to score again, only for the opportunity to take something from the game to pass them by, with Fàbregas adding a third goal for Arsenal in stoppage time to make the scoreline suggest an afternoon that turned out to be far more comfortable for Arsène Wenger's side than it was.

Liverpool's defeat at Highbury was their 11th on the road in the Premier League in 2004/05 and it meant that from a possible maximum of 57 points that could have been obtained on their travels, Benítez's side procured just 18, which was as many as 14th-placed Blackburn Rovers claimed and fewer than the four teams that would roll over the finish line directly behind Liverpool: Bolton Wanderers, Middlesbrough, Manchester City, and Tottenham Hotspur.

Another away loss it had been, but positives could be taken from their second-half performance, especially that of Cissé, who proved a far more potent threat than Baroš had during a first half in which his first touch consistently let him down. With a final-day game at home to Aston Villa offering the only chance for a full 90-minute run out for the French international ahead of the trip to Istanbul, Benítez suddenly had a conundrum to ponder, a question further underlined by the fact that Baroš had gone over two months since his last goal.

Three days before the Arsenal game the Football Association had finally clarified their position on Champions League qualification for the 2005/06 season, with no provision being given for the fourth-placed team making way for Liverpool should they defeat Milan in the final. Within 24 hours of defeat at Highbury consigning Benítez's team the potential of being denied the right to defend the trophy they would be duelling over in Istanbul, Lennart Johansson, the UEFA president, aired noises intimating that a remedy to such a scenario would need to be found should Liverpool overcome Milan, but that he was willing to wait and see if the hypothetical would become reality first.

Clear, without being crystal clear, UEFA had at least left the door to the 2005/06 Champions League ajar for Liverpool, but as part of his musings Johansson had stated that European football's governing body would also need to take steps to leave no ambiguities in the future over their requirement for the Champions League winners to defend the prize the following season. Meanwhile, in additional upbeat news, while UEFA had drawn Liverpool as the away team for the final, Milan's preference of playing in all white meant that Benítez's team would be taking to the pitch in all red, with both clubs being pleased to be in colours that had served them well in European Cup and Champions League finals of the past.

With the Premier League season just days away from ending, the transfer rumour mill began to crank into gear once again, with the Deportivo de La Coruña president Augusto César Lendoiro, feeling the need to refute links to Liverpool for the Argentine defensive midfielder Aldo Duscher and the Spanish international attacker Albert Luque; the latter would eventually spend a misfiring two years with Newcastle United instead.

Travel plans and the acquiring of tickets falling into place, beyond fourth position in the Premier League drifting out of reach after the loss to Arsenal, a strange footballing ether materialised as Liverpool bided their time before the final. The transfer rumour mill was certainly one way to pass the time, with Luís Figo's name being mentioned causing a stir, while conversation among supporters also circulated around the topic of Benítez's team selection dilemmas, plus which players the club would be waving goodbye to in the summer. It was as if the impending visit of Aston Villa to Anfield was a distraction that many could have done without, and with a week and a half still to go until facing Milan, while excitement levels were rising, patience was in short supply.

Dietmar Hamann, the subject of interest from Bolton and out of contract at the end of June, was happy to defer any decision on his future until after the events of Istanbul had played themselves out, while Vladimír Šmicer had already been informed that his contract was not going to be renewed, making for two unhappy Czech Republic internationals with Baroš airing his frustrations over the regularity of how often he was being substituted during games.

It was a poor sense of timing for Baroš to be making such observations as against Aston Villa, Benítez handed a first start since his return from injury to Cissé, upon which he more than grabbed the opportunity to make his manager's choice of striker a more considered one that it might have been for the final. Two first-half goals, the first from the penalty spot and the second being swept past the Danish international goalkeeper Thomas Sørensen after an Antonio Núñez cut-back; in the Anfield sunshine, an often-troubled Premier League campaign ended on a bright note.

With starts also having been handed to Scott Carson, Josemi, Mauricio Pellegrino, Stephen Warnock, and Anthony Le Tallec along with Bišćan, Núñez, and Kewell, only the inclusions of Jamie Carragher, Riise, and Alonso seemed to represent a definitive gamble by Benítez in terms of the 11 players that would be taking to the pitch at the Atatürk, and it would have been to his relief that no new injuries were sustained on an afternoon when Jerzy Dudek, Steve Finnan, Sami Hyypiä, Hamann, and Baroš were all stood down to the bench, while Djimi Traoré, Gerrard, and García were not on duty at all.

Cissé completed the full 90 minutes, with Kewell being given an hour before being replaced by Baroš, Benítez using the game to indulge in an experiment or two, with Kewell seemingly energised by the presence of Cissé sufficiently enough to display a few of the skills that the Anfield faithful had seen mostly lay dormant across the span of the season. Hamann was also thrown on for the final 20 minutes, as if given the late run to further attune himself to the wavelength of Alonso.

A win on the final day, but not without a flutter in the stomach when Aston Villa came back into the game during the second half, with Gareth Barry reducing Liverpool's lead with over 20 minutes left to play, during which Riise thundered a shot against Sørensen's crossbar while Carson was forced to watch on as a Luke Moore header bounced back off his.

Victory for Liverpool was enough to secure them fifth place in the Premier League table, with Champions League Final anticipation offset by frustration that a top-four place domestically had been beyond them when it really shouldn't have been. Benítez's side had finished three points behind Everton, but with David Moyes's team having lost their final two fixtures, their penultimate match ending in a 7-0 defeat at Highbury against Arsenal, the numbers game suggested that Liverpool had only themselves to blame for their fate.

Liverpool had scored more goals and conceded fewer than Everton and ended the season with a goal difference that was 12 better off than their neighbours, who had even finished with a negative goal difference. Lessons were clearly there to be learned domestically by Benítez, but they were considerations that could wait until the summer. All eyes were now firmly locked on Istanbul.

For Liverpool, a relatively sedate 11 days sat between the Aston Villa game and the Champions League Final. Meanwhile, Carlo Ancelotti's Milan had the distraction of trying to keep their Serie A title hopes alive after a 2-2 draw away to Lecce, on the same day the Premier League season came to an end, had left *I Rossoneri* five points behind Juventus with only two games to play, this from having led the race on goal difference with four left.

All had seemed rosy for Milan as April came to an end. In Serie A, they had dropped just four points across a 13-game span since the beginning of February, while in the Champions League knockout rounds they had consummately eased Manchester United out of the tournament in the last 16 before outclassing Internazionale in that explosive quarter-final in which the second leg was prematurely curtailed because of crowd disorder.

Leading 3-0 on aggregate at the time, UEFA went on to award Milan a 3-0 win for the second leg which gave them a 5-0 aggregate success, with Ancelotti's side progressing to a semi-final showdown against Guus Hiddink's PSV Eindhoven, where a 90th-minute strike by Jon Dahl Tomasson in the San Siro first leg edged Milan to a 2-0 victory that put them in a strong position when heading to the Philips Stadion for the return game, 24 hours after Liverpool had clinched their place in the final.

Given that Milan had kept nine clean sheets across the 11 Champions League games they had played throughout 2004/05 up to that point, in Eindhoven they were fast approaching 11 hours of football since they had last conceded in the tournament when Park Ji-sung enlivened matters with a ninth-minute opener for PSV, to draw his side to within one goal on aggregate, while 25 minutes were still on the clock when Phillip Cocu levelled proceedings in the second half.

Here lay for all to see a sudden frailty within the seemingly impenetrable Milan rearguard, and it was only when Massimo Ambrosini put a glancing header past Heurelho Gomes that the game was put beyond PSV, although Cocu was to score again a minute later, to render their visitors panic-stricken once more, until the final whistle came to their rescue.

Promisingly for Liverpool, 13 months earlier Milan had already displayed an unease with being pressured when footballing convention might suggest a win was theirs in all but name, when blowing a 4-1 first-leg advantage in the 2003/04 Champions League quarter-finals, against Deportivo de La Coruña, swept away by a 4-0 defeat at the Estadio Riazor in which they were 3-0 down by half-time. Perhaps, beneath the skill, sophistication, defensive strength, midfield mastery, and attacking potency of Milan, lay a soft underbelly that struggled to stomach an unexpected powerplay flowing towards them.

Four days beyond their close shave in Eindhoven, Milan were beaten at home by Juventus in a crucial Serie A clash, the only goal of the game being scored by David

Trezeguet, and a week later they twice relinquished the lead to drop two more points in that 2-2 draw at Lecce. Beginning with the loss over 90 minutes at PSV, Milan would fail to win any of their last six games of the season, with both prizes that they were aiming for stunningly slipping from their grasp.

With a week to go until the final, Milan still seemed like they were both the hard place and the immovable force, however, opponents whose most recent Champions League success had come just two years earlier when defeating Juventus on penalties at Old Trafford after a goalless 120 minutes. Since Liverpool had last been the champions of Europe, Milan had been crowned as such on four further occasions, while twice losing the final. In some respects it felt like the Reds were going into the ring with Mike Tyson and doing so without a gum shield. Benítez was no Trevor Berbick, however.

Ancelotti was positively effusive about the organisational capabilities of his opposite number, with Tim Rich of the *Daily Telegraph* taking a trip to Milan for some pre-final reconnaissance, quoting the former Italian international midfielder over his admiration for the way the Liverpool manager could structure his defence, 'Benítez is a very defensive coach but defending well is a quality, not a defect.' Ancelotti went on to state that he would not be surprised if the game went to a penalty shoot-out, yet he could not have foreseen the reason why his semi-prediction would come to pass.

Just like Ancelotti, Paolo Maldini, the Milan captain, was also glowing in his praise of Liverpool's defensive unit, impressed as he was especially by Carragher, yet where his coach was not drawn on talk about the perceived lack of attacking threat of the Benítez method, Maldini was happy to expound on his thoughts, as although he conceded that 'once Liverpool go ahead, they are dangerous because it becomes hard to find space to break them down, especially if you are not playing all that brilliantly', he also stated that Milan knew how to attack, whereas their opponents had caution at the heart of their game.

From Maldini, it was an insightful and blunt assessment. He was under no illusion that Milan would be facing the Champions League version of Liverpool rather than the Premier League variety, but he also struck an air of supreme confidence that he and his team-mates would be too strong for their opponents, and that they would be intelligent enough to avoid the pitfalls that Juventus had been caught out by during the quarter-finals.

On the Friday before facing Liverpool, Milan's now slim Serie A title hopes were ended when being held to a 3-3 draw at home to Palermo after letting a 3-1 half-time lead drift. At face value, the result appears to be a chilling prophesy of the fate that would envelope Milan the following Wednesday in Istanbul, yet only one player who was involved in the 18 named by Ancelotti in this game would go on to find themselves in the starting line-up for the Champions League Final – Hernán Crespo. Indeed, so altered a team did Ancelotti field against Palermo that four of the starting 11 didn't even make the bench five days later.

All eggs now in their Champions League basket, the Milan line-up largely selected itself for the final, with the only ambiguity to linger being the question of whether or not Crespo would start given that the goals had dried up for him since he had been the hero in both legs of their last-16 home and away victories over Manchester United, in which he was the sole goalscorer each time in the absence of Andriy Shevchenko.

With only two goals to his name across the two and a half months since the second leg against United, Crespo had sat inactive on the bench for Milan in the second leg of the semi-final against PSV and the crucial Serie A clash with Juventus four days later.

At the Philips Stadion, Ancelotti had opted to draft in Ambrosini to midfield, with Clarence Seedorf occasionally pushing up to supplement Shevchenko and Kaká, and when things began to go awry it was to Tomasson that Ancelotti turned, rather than Crespo, with the Danish international then being preferred to start the Juventus game too.

By the time the Palermo match came around, with Crespo and Tomasson starting, the fixture had basically taken on the air of the two of them auditioning for the start alongside Shevchenko in Istanbul, and with a goal and the full 90 minutes to his name it was Tomasson who looked the better bet on a day when Crespo was withdrawn midway through the second half. Added to this, Tomasson had climbed from the bench during the first leg of the semi-final to score that ultimately critical injury-time second goal.

Within this battle between Crespo and Tomasson, the alternative option of Ambrosini had been subtracted from the equation by the injury that had ended his participation in the Lecce game at half-time and unwittingly brought his season to an early end too. Yet, this one conundrum aside, the Milan starting line-up fell quite effortlessly into place, with Dida in goal behind a back four of Maldini, Cafu, Alessandro Nesta, and Jaap Stam, a midfield of Seedorf, Andrea Pirlo, and Gennaro Gattuso, while the winner of the Crespo and Tomasson decision would team up in attack with Shevchenko and Kaká.

Benítez and his squad touched down in Istanbul 48 hours ahead of the game, with the manager seemingly juggling a similar poser to the one Ancelotti had on his hands. Whereas the Italian was, at least on the outside looking in, pondering a choice between Crespo and Tomasson, for Benítez it all appeared to be a question of who would lead the line, be it Baroš or Cissé, with the smart money drifting toward it being the latter rather than the former.

Cissé's two goals against Aston Villa as part of a full 90-minute run-out had made him the more attractive proposition compared to Baroš, the extra kick of pace that the former Auxerre man possessed being viewed as a powerful weapon against a Milan defence whose collective age weighed in at a shade under 134 years old. Meanwhile, all other ten starting spots seemed set in stone, with Dudek behind a settled back four of Finnan, Traoré, Carragher, and Hyypiä, supporting a midfield of Alonso, Hamann, Riise, and García, with Gerrard sitting in behind either Baroš or Cissé. Benítez, the organised, but flexible pragmatist, had a shock in store, however.

On the eve of the final the grapevine began to whisper with word that Kewell might just be a shock inclusion in the starting 11 at the expense of Hamann, with Gerrard operating in midfield alongside Alonso, rather than in the hole behind what was still widely expected to be Cissé. In the Milan camp, all signs were starting to point towards Crespo getting the nod from Ancelotti, ahead of Tomasson.

As the travelling red side of Merseyside, and Liverpool's wider supporter base beyond, descended upon Istanbul, also holding court in any enclave that sat within striking distance of the Bosphorus, an extended party vibe encircled the location of the final. There was a defined mission to enjoy the ride for the supporters, but for the manager, his coaching staff, and the players, there was a trophy to be won, and despite the underdog role that they occupied there was no reason that the impossible couldn't become the possible.

When the day of the game finally dawned, most rumours over the composition of Benítez's starting line-up proved to be entirely founded, with Kewell's name indeed present, although the talk of Cissé starting ahead of Baroš proved to be wide of the mark, while Warnock was to be the devastated 19th man, the player to miss out completely on the squad, not even afforded a place among the substitutes.

Gerrard, the man set to lead Liverpool on to the pitch at the Atatürk Olympic Stadium, was high on imagination as the game drew near, stating in the build-up that he could imagine lifting the European Cup, that he could imagine assuming his place in an Anfield pantheon of legends, that he longed for a picture of himself holding aloft that big trophy with the looping handles, to join the wall at Anfield upon which the legendary faces of the past doing just that resided.

Anticipation was understandably high, among the travelling supporters and within the squad too. Here lay the biggest game in the life of a generation that hadn't been lucid to the successes of the 1970s and 1980s, and one for those who did live those days to place alongside the glories of Rome 1977, Wembley 1978, Paris 1981, and Rome 1984.

A day bathed in glorious sunshine, rolled through to a balmy evening and the business of the Champions League Final, a communion in red, that had an elaborate opening ceremony to endure, which in terms of a celebration of the day wasn't a patch on the carnival that Liverpool's supporters had created for themselves, either at Taksim Square or outside the stadium.

Constructing the most incredible bubble for the game to take place in, apart from the end where all the goals would be scored, the Atatürk was an ocean of red and white, a visage that wasn't lost on the Liverpool players as they warmed up. Watching on from my vantage point, I spotted a moment shared between Carragher and García, where the former put an arm around the shoulder of the latter before sweeping his other arm around three quarters of the stadium, as if to point out where the fans were. A shake of the head from García, who then jogged over to Alonso, where he put an arm around the shoulder of the midfielder before sweeping his other arm around three quarters of the stadium, relaying what he had been told by Carragher.

Preliminaries over, it was almost as if Liverpool were enjoying themselves so much that they forgot there was a game of football to take part in as Paolo Maldini gave Milan the lead with only 53 seconds having elapsed, volleying past Dudek after connecting with an Andrea Pirlo free kick conceded by Traoré, the ball being arrowed into the penalty area from the right. As starts go, it could hardly have been a worse one for Liverpool. Before long, Crespo came close to a second goal for Milan, with García the unlikely goal-line clearing hero, while at the other end Hyypiä gave Dida his first piece of food for thought.

For Liverpool, more turbulence was to come as midway through the first half it became evident that the Kewell gamble had failed and he limped from the scene with a groin strain, to be replaced by Šmicer, with Benítez opting against bringing Hamann on to provide extra security to an increasingly besieged midfield.

Overrun and off-balance, Liverpool were caught within a first-half maelstrom, with Kaká, Shevchenko, and Crespo stretching Benítez's defence to its very limits, the through balls of Kaká wreaking consummate damage. Just before the half-hour, Shevchenko got on the end of one such pass, planting the ball past Dudek, only for Liverpool to be saved by the linesman's flag.

Ten minutes later, Milan would have their second goal, hitting Liverpool on the break with precision via a move that began with a penalty claim from García when the ball struck the arm of Nesta, as he went to ground in the Milan 18-yard-box. Shouts waved away, Kaká took possession, carrying the ball forward, before finding Shevchenko on the right, who cut it across to a falling Crespo, who was able to turn it home past the exposed Dudek. The thrust of Ancelotti's team was ruthless and Liverpool were without an answer to it.

All that Benítez's men could do at this point was to get themselves to the interval without absorbing more damage. Yet even that was to prove too much to hope for, as with only one more minute to navigate until half-time, Kaká slipped Gerrard, moved himself into space, and then sent a sumptuous through ball that evaded the desperate attempts to intercept of Carragher, with Crespo taking the pass in his stride before clipping it past the advancing Dudek and into the net for 3-0.

Shock and awe. Into the dressing room Liverpool's players stumbled, where a myriad of tangents took place, as Carragher remembers it, 'It was a bit chaotic when we got back in the dressing room. Everyone was playing the biggest game of their lives, everyone's heads are down. You think it's over. Rafa Benítez is not a motivator, he's someone who can change games tactically, he's certainly not going to lift everyone in the dressing room. It's just not his way. Yes, he could get his message across, but it wouldn't flow, it wasn't just off the cuff, where he would get emotional.'

Going further, Carragher spoke of the confusion at play, 'The first thing he did, he told Djimi Traoré to go get a shower. Rather than explaining to someone why they were coming off at half-time, the changes he was going to make, he'd just say "shower", so he just said, "Traoré, shower," and that was quite blunt.'

While this was going on, a problem was arising concerning Finnan. A difference of opinion between player and physio bubbled up. Ever observant, Carragher noted, 'Next thing, Steve Finnan and the physio are having a debate, Finnan thinks he can carry on, physio didn't think he'd last for the second half. Benítez then gets told this and thinks, "Oh god, I've just thrown Djimi Traoré off, I've already used one sub in the first half." Then he tells Traoré to get out the shower and Finnan goes in the shower. We changed to three at the back, Didi Hamann comes back in because he'd been out warming up. Rafa has to then put it all on the board and write what we're going to do. He actually put 12 men on – he put Djibril Cissé on there as well so, for whatever reason, Djibril had his tracksuit top off. That brought a little smile to our faces even at half-time.'

Sharp in clarity about what was happening in wider terms in the dressing room at half-time, directly around him, matters were more of a fog to Carragher, 'Sometimes you feel like you want to go back. What did actually happen in those 15 minutes? I'm not sure what conversations I was having with Stevie or other people and how they were reacting. It was chaotic and it wasn't a normal 15 minutes. It all adds to the miracle of Istanbul.

Everyone has their own way of seeing things, or how that half-time went. Djibril Cissé believed that Stevie did the team talk and Rafa Benítez was sent outside. I remember him saying that years ago – it was nonsense.'

Out on the terraces of the Atatürk there was a stunned sense of solemnity among the Liverpool supporters, but the strains of 'You'll Never Walk Alone', that began almost in the form of a funeral hymn, soon grew and grew in velocity, sang slowly, yet with a rich defiance at its heart. The message seemed to be that while we might have been falling apart, we were more than willing to do it together.

Back on to the pitch Liverpool's players strode for the second half, Hamann at last joining the fray, Finnan withdrawn, Traoré reprieved from the shower, a formation altered, and Benítez down two of his three substitutes already. A mountainous task lay in front of the team in all red if they were to even claw a modicum of respectability back, let alone put themselves in with a chance of turning the final on its head. The one thing that Liverpool did have in their favour, however, was that the second half at least represented a fresh start, a blank sheet of paper to try and sketch something out that was more cohesive and recognisable than what they had scrawled in the first half.

Upon the resumption, it was still Milan initially probing for further goals, Dudek being tested on a couple of occasions, but in the 56th minute came the first step in a dramatic shift in direction as a Riise cross from the left, at the second time of asking, was headed beyond a startled Dida by Gerrard to reduce Liverpool's arrears to two goals.

It prompted celebrations from the travelling Liverpool supporters that bordered on relief, as opposed to delirium, although there was still an air of loose resignation of a probable defeat circulating at this point. There was liberation in Gerrard's goal, a moment that eased the shoulders a little, a flash of positivity that made an impending annihilation at least more likely to be a less bruising loss. A touch of self-respect had been restored, and with well over half an hour to go, you never know, we might just snatch another one back towards the end of the game.

Two minutes beyond Gerrard's goal, the concept of a mission in the name of aiming for a more noble form of defeat was thrown completely out of the window as when the ball arrived at the feet of Šmicer from Hamann, his low shot from distance caught Dida out, as the Milan goalkeeper got his attempt to parry all wrong. Astonishingly, the ball was nestling in the back of the net once more, and this time, the Liverpool supporters in attendance were lost within a sea of delirium, Šmicer himself setting off on a celebration that was almost Tardelli-esqe.

Adrenalin pumping on the pitch and on the terraces for those who were at the Atatürk in the name of Liverpool, for Milan there was only an increasing state of panic, Ancelotti's team now needing to assimilate events that made no sense at all to them while also trying to put the genie back in the bottle.

If Gerrard's goal had been a foot in the door, Šmicer's had been an axe through the wood panelling, and all that remained left to do now was to take it off the hinges. Three minutes later, after being laid on by Baroš, Gerrard broke into the Milan penalty area only to be pulled back by Gennaro Gattuso. Manuel Mejuto González, the Spanish referee, pointed to the penalty spot. Liverpool had been presented with an opportunity to complete the unthinkable. They had the chance to level the scoreline.

Rather than Gerrard stepping up to take the penalty, instead of Baroš being handed the responsibility it was quite the shock to see Alonso with the ball tucked under his arm. A nod of his head, a determined run-up, and a low shot to Dida's right, there was a collective sharp intake of breath when the Brazilian international made the save, only for bedlam to erupt as the net bulged to the tune of Alonso forcing home the rebound.

A mass of red and white humanity, tumbling up, down, and across the terraces of the Atatürk made for a staggering backdrop to the joy and despair unfolding on the pitch. These had been the most incredible five and a half minutes in the history of Liverpool Football Club, and there was still to be another hour to play, along with the tension of a penalty shoot-out to come.

From humiliation to elation, there was never going to be any stopping Liverpool from this point onward. A battle of wits, a war of attrition, call it what you will, but Benítez's team were not for buckling, and with stubborn resistance at the heart of every tackle, every block, every save, the more that the Reds' belief grew, the more Milan's soul shrunk.

Traoré's goal-line clearance, Dudek's double save from Shevchenko, Gerrard dropping back and wide in extra time to neutralise the threat of Serginho, Carragher fighting through cramp, it was with belligerence and a near pig-headedness that Liverpool dragged the matter to 120 minutes and beyond. A resolve not to fold; the fresh legs of Cissé for the last 35 minutes were invaluable to the cause.

As the outcome eventually boiled down to a shoot-out, Carragher was zeroed in on Dudek prior to the first kick being taken, imparting words of wisdom about how Bruce Grobbelaar had psyched out Roma's spot-kick takers during the 1984 European Cup Final. By now, Dudek was in a zone all of his own making. After that double save so late in extra time, nothing could possibly faze him.

Over the crossbar Serginho sent his kick, and Pirlo stepped up to see his effort saved, as Hamann and Cissé converted for Liverpool. For some of us on the terraces, the tears were already flowing. Tomasson then got Milan on the board, and when Riise saw his penalty saved by Dida, Kaká was able to apply some pressure by levelling matters at 2-2.

Suddenly there was a sense of peril at play as Šmicer made the long walk, the knowledge that should he miss then Liverpool's advantage would be truly blown swirling in the minds of all watching on. The player himself, however, was coolness personified. He sent Dida the wrong way and planted the ball into the net with negligible fuss. Now it was all down to Shevchenko and Dudek. Who would flinch?

Wide-eyed and apprehensive as he made his approach to the spot, Shevchenko wasn't for locking his sightline directly with that of Dudek as he looked to the referee first, and then towards the dumbstruck Milan supporters behind the goal. No longer able to delay his date with destiny, the Ukrainian legend took a leaden run-up before striking the ball straight down the middle, where Dudek was able to bat it away with his left hand.

Ecstatic shockwaves reverberated around three-quarters of the terraces of the Atatürk, while in the Milan section there was only desolation. A fine football club had played an indelible part of a legendary night, and in so many respects, it was bewildering that they weren't going home with the trophy.

Dudek's save from Shevchenko was to be the cure of aching limbs and fatigued bodies as his team-mates, previously congregated on the halfway line, set off to envelope him in celebration, converging on him with jet-heeled abandon. The spring was very much back in the step of the club as the after-show party got into full swing.

Medals adorned around necks, trophy handed over by Lennart Johansson, Gerrard thrust the prize into the Istanbul night sky as the cannon blasts of confetti turned the vista redder than ever. It all felt so surreal to be a part of the football history that had just unfolded, yet it also felt so very, very right.

Against all the odds, the miracle had been successfully performed.

Chapter Fourteen

Once in a Lifetime

IT ISN'T just the journey on that green bus from Taksim Square to the Atatürk Olympic Stadium that stays in the mind. There was also the green bus journey from the stadium to Sabiha Gökçen airport after we finally drifted away from the scene of the greatest crime in Champions League Final history.

Alan and his son Greg were meant to be on the flight out of Manchester Airport directly prior to myself, Big Andy, Sue, Martin, Gary, Anthony, Stevie and Alison, and their boys. The plan was that they would wait at arrivals for us, and we would be able to share the day with them. That was undone when Alan and Greg's flight was delayed, and we instead took off first.

With no idea of when Alan and Greg would be arriving at Sabiha Gökçen, all we could do upon our own arrival was to jump on one of the coaches that were ferrying Liverpool supporters to Taksim Square and hope that they would catch up with us later on. The day progressed, the evening came, the Champions League was won, and out of the Atatürk we stumbled to our pre-arranged meeting point, to dispense hugs, and wipe moist eyes. There was still no Alan and Greg. Had they even made it to Istanbul?

Those green buses. There they were, lined up with placards in the front window denoting where their journey was heading. Thousands upon thousands of football supporters, this phalanx of green buses, and a loose smattering of young Turkish men who were handed the job of directing human traffic. Ignoring the flawed system, we all ambled past and checked the front window of each bus until we found one with the desired destination.

Our emerald chariot filled up, the driver closed the doors and off we set, without getting too far due to a job lot of other buses all trying to take to the road in all too quick succession. From here, a game of musical buses began in earnest as some passengers belatedly realised that they were on a bus heading to a different location to the one they needed to reach. For those who hadn't been lucky enough to get on a bus, they were steaming through the static traffic in a bid to reach the road with the hope of flagging down a taxi. It was chaos, UEFA style.

As one or two passengers alighted our bus, it meant there was a small amount of space for fresh arrivals. A speculative knock on the door and on jumped a dad and his lad. With much amusement, we realised it was Alan and Greg. They could have gatecrashed any of the numerous buses that were heading to Sabiha Gökçen, but they went and climbed on to ours.

With Alan and Greg situated at the front of the bus, next to the driver, we maintained a series of shouted conversations from our seats, around half the way back, and eventually the wheels started to roll. Unfortunately the driver didn't seem to know where he was meant to be going, as we drifted past motorway exits for Sabiha Gökçen.

Suspiciously, we seemed to be following signs back to Taksim Square, which was when Alan stepped in with attempted navigation advice for a driver who didn't speak a word of English, our plucky hero resorting to a rudimentary form of sign language by doing his best impression of an airplane. To be fair to Alan, the driver seemed to understand, and a good 45 minutes or so later we were making our approach to the airport.

Within this, there was just one problem. We were approaching the wrong airport. Rather than rolling up at Sabiha Gökçen, we were heading towards Atatürk Airport. We weren't even in the Asian part of Istanbul at this point. Our journey to the correct airport would take the best part of another two hours, and when we got there, we were walking into a dehydrated and chaotic landscape where the departure lounge was a makeshift tented edifice.

With flight numbers that didn't fully correspond between what was printed on the ticket and what was being displayed on the departure boards, the result was that we were sat on the runway in a half-full airplane for almost as long as we were on that green bus that had taken us on a scenic route from the stadium to eventually the correct airport.

A test of endurance; this was why we never made it on to the streets of Liverpool for the team's homecoming, yet despite the mental and physical toll of a day that would stretch to roughly 60 hours from leaving the house to putting the key back in the latch again the party rarely subsided, and when it did lull it was never long before it kicked back into motion. Through the fatigue, it would dawn on us again and again just what had unfolded in that stadium that looked as if it had been constructed on the face of the moon in a location that felt like it was a million miles away from downtown Istanbul.

Shared experiences, a familiar knowledge, even all this time later, upon any occasion when you get into a conversation with somebody who was also at the 2005 Champions League Final, or at any of those unforgettable Anfield nights along the route to Istanbul, the glow is a mutually warm one. There is a bespoke and knowing smile at play, and we all have our stories to tell.

Nick Burgess managed to find his way on to the pitch after the game, lingering long enough to score goals of his own with a tennis ball, before working his way into the press box where he rubbed shoulders with Phil Thompson and Franz Beckenbauer and ended up purchasing a Champions League jacket from a UEFA official.

Chris Thomas remembers the locals lining the streets along the route to the stadium in scenes that were akin to the levels of encroachment spectators of the mountain stages of the Tour de France insist upon making, while the lost Shankly boy, George Scott, shared the trip with his son Gavin; George never lost hope, even at 3-0 down, with Shankly's mantra to 'never give up' at the forefront of his mind.

Author Keith Salmon undertook a six-day odyssey involving five flights, four train journeys, and a walk across a dodgy border crossing, to a town where nobody spoke a word of English, in Alan Whicker-like experiences that inspired him to write a book of his own. In a similar theme, Keith Wagstaff's journey took in six flights and one train, with Köln being the pivot point of the trip, the same city where Rafael Benítez stumbled into a bar full of Liverpool fans, to become an automatic accidental hero.

Ian Ford and his cousin opted to go at the 11th hour, moving from hotel to hotel across three nights, only to see their return flight cancelled, leaving them another £500 out of pocket each in order to secure themselves alternative tickets, while Craig Georgeson did the final via Bulgaria, inclusive of a ten-hour road trip that meandered up and down countless hills along the way.

Phil Roose had to oversee a late mate of his being extricated from a boat on the Bosphorus by the Red Crescent after dislocating his hip. While his mate and concerned lady friend missed the game, heading off instead to hospital, Phil exchanged one of the suddenly available tickets for a crate of Efes, while he later sold the other unused one on eBay, still making a profit on the face value.

Kirsty Watson was threatened with assault at the Atatürk as she dared to join in with the singing of 'You'll Never Walk Alone' at half-time, when an irate gang of lads took exception to the backing the team were being afforded in the wake of a shocker of a first half, while Eddie Starrs stuck it out, despite his two mates being among the trickle of supporters who opted to head back to the centre of Istanbul at half-time.

John O'Dwyer, as so many people do in such footballing moments, shared anxieties and humour with the stranger stood at his side at the start of extra time, a man who was desperate that the game wouldn't go to penalties only to declare his newfound love of the shoot-out system after Jerzy Dudek's heroics.

When Neil Wilkes and three of his friends came to arrange their travel plans, one of their party opted out of the idea of doing the three-night trip as he had nobody to look after the dog, and instead went for the day journey. As the game went onward to extra time and penalties, rolling itself into the following day, his flight took off without him, marooning him in Istanbul until he could book an alternative seat to Bristol, from where he had to take a coach back to Liverpool.

Best plans laid to waste, in the end Neil and the other two who had done the three-day trip were out of the country for around three hours fewer than their day-tripping mate was. Having crossed paths at the airport, Neil had rounded up all the Turkish currency they had left between the three of them and handed it over to the solo traveller, along with a job lot of Mars bars. In further news of misadventure, Lee McLoughlin managed to lose his phone in the wide expanse of Istanbul, only for a couple of his mates, who were in different accommodation and on alternative flights, to find it.

Then there was Paul Salt, presenter of the *Total Sport* show on BBC Radio Merseyside and in May 2005 an integral part of the Radio City *Breakfast Show*. The 2004/05 season was the first that Paul was able to indulge in travelling to European aways, and he took in the trips to Monaco, Bayer Leverkusen, Juventus, Chelsea, and Istanbul.

Paul spoke of being unable to find an establishment in Monte Carlo that would serve only drinks, instead being expected to purchase food too, circumnavigating the problem by ordering ten bottles of lager and a plate of chips; in Köln he was in the Jameson Distillery on the evening that Rafael Benítez ambled in with Pako Ayestarán. A photo of Paul and Benítez went viral across regional and national newspapers.

They were not all great experiences; Paul was also in Turin for the gauntlet run into the Stadio Delle Alpi, driving in from a base camp some ten to 15 miles away via the splendour of Lake Como. If events inside the stadium hadn't been unsettling enough, he and his friends were panicked when, on the way out and back to their vehicle, they momentarily thought their hire car was ablaze, before being relieved to see that it was the car they'd parked next to instead. This was set against a familial landscape where his wife-to-be and parents had implored him to give Turin a miss.

For Istanbul, Paul was offered the opportunity by Radio City to go on a working remit, flying out with the Liverpool team on the Monday, co-presenting on air live from the Atatürk on the morning of the game, and getting a sneak preview in just how far the stadium is from downtown Istanbul, while the rest of us remained blissfully ignorant.

Watching on from a press box that collectively dropped all pretence of professionalism, Paul and his fellow journalists were as wrapped up in the game as everyone else was, and he greatly enjoyed the media after-match party that was put on in his hotel, celebrating with John Aldridge and Gary Gillespie when he spotted one glum-faced individual. When Paul went over to enquire if he was OK, the supporter confessed that he was delighted that Liverpool had won, but that he had been one of those souls that had departed the scene at half-time, and his taxi driver had been breaking news of each Liverpool goal to him as best he could.

Cherry on the cake for Paul? On the same flight as the Liverpool team once again on the way back to John Lennon Airport, instead of being at the back where all the members of the media had been on the way out, there was an impromptu sit-where-you-like system in operation, leading to him and Steve Hothersall, the Radio City match commentator, sitting near Sami Hyypiä, where the champagne and trophy was passed around for all to enjoy.

Back on Merseyside, as the team headed for the open-top bus, Paul was sent to St George's Hall to broadcast on the parade. With little in the way of time to recover, the following day he was off to Madrid for his stag do.

Not everyone made it to the final who might have done. Steve Hales, a regular at home and away games, lacked the foresight that Istanbul was a realistic possibility and booked a family holiday, beginning 25 May, even contriving to be airborne while the game was taking place, although reaching his coach transfer in time to phone home so that his sister could provide him a running commentary of the penalty shoot-out – at great expense to his mobile phone bill.

Joy unconfined, memories banked, Istanbul and the 2005 Champions League Final was all about the shared nature of it. Magical moments collected with the very best of people, but this was also just the culmination of a mission. There had been many such moments along the run, with Rob Storry citing the second leg of the semi-final and what he considers to be the greatest Anfield atmosphere he has ever experienced. Rob started queueing for his semi-final ticket at 5.30am, so intent he was to procure a spot right in the middle of the Kop. On the night of the game, Walton Breck Road was bouncing to a carnival mood hours before kick-off.

From that semi-final night, I can remember the walk back to the car, and all the doors of the houses having been flung wide open with residents taking to their doorsteps to be part of the celebrations, to drink it all in. I must have hugged every single one of them along the way, while down at Stamford Bridge at the first leg, what has never left me is the esoteric argument that took place at the turnstiles when either Tomasz Radzinski, or someone who looked very much like Tomasz Radzinski, was rounded on by one Liverpool supporter for having the temerity of either being, or looking like, the former

Everton striker, only to be embraced wildly by everyone else because he was there to support Reds.

Still to this day, I have no idea if it was Tomasz Radzinski or not, although he was by then playing his football for Fulham, so he would have been in the vicinity. On the way home we stopped at Watford Gap services, where I ran a lap of honour after winning something cheap and flammable on the grabber machine, completely taking the passing Arsenal defender Philippe Senderos by surprise.

The author Jeff Goulding declares that the second leg against Chelsea was the greatest Anfield night he has ever experienced, with the Olympiacos game a close second, the comeback against the Greek champions having had an almost supernatural inevitability to its outcome, especially during those last 20 minutes.

Yet Chelsea was different, according to Jeff, 'It was a game laced with jeopardy, and only raw human energy got us through. In both this and the Olympiacos game though, the atmosphere was simply incredible. But the noise in the semi-final was on a different level altogether. We all got into the ground early and by half-time few of us had voices left. We had shredded our vocal cords with a constant barrage of noise. Every time Chelsea touched the ball they were booed, and we ran through every song in the Kop's playbook. That game epitomised everything about the Benítez era. Grit, belief, determination, a little flair, a ruthless commitment to the plan – in the stands and on the pitch – and yes, a bit of luck too. The noise that greeted the final whistle and Liverpool's return to the pinnacle of European football will live with me until my dying day. The Reds were back, Chelsea had been vanquished, and all of European football would sit up and take notice. It was absolutely about the power of Anfield, yes, but the man who lit the fuse that season was Rafa Benítez.'

Jeff didn't make it to Istanbul, and watched the final at home, where the first-half lesson handed out by Milan and the trauma of those first 45 minutes prompted him to step outside to compose himself, 'As I stood there, I noticed that on the doorstep of nearly all the houses in my street were men and women contemplating the same dilemma as me. Should we turn off our televisions and go to bed or face the second half? With a nod to the man and son standing outside the door opposite to mine, I went back inside to tough out the second half. What followed was the greatest fightback I have ever seen and I wept at the end.'

Prior to all of this, of course, was the visit of Juventus for the first leg of the quarter-final, for which I helped lay out the mosaic, the designer of these things being my best mate Big Andy, the same Big Andy who was stunned when he descended from that green bus outside the Atatürk to find that I was sat on a stone wall enquiring what had kept them, when they all thought I was a few miles back down the road, marooned in the mountainous hill roads.

Meanwhile, that Juventus game sparked a two-decade-long difference of opinion between Paul Moran and his son over whether or not Gianluigi Buffon managed to get a hand to Luis García's shot for Liverpool's second goal that night. Many years later, and still a hot topic of conversation in the Moran household, they even put it out to a Twitter poll, where the findings were 51-49 per cent in favour of Buffon not getting a glove on the ball. Paul still refutes the close outcome of the vote.

Breaking the fourth wall, Istanbul even reached out of the television screen and spoke to plenty of non-Liverpool supporters, general lovers of football who just happen to follow other teams yet still found themselves being swept up by the drama that was unfolding.

Andy Abbott, a Leeds United fan, watched the game in a Leeds bar with a Liverpool-supporting workmate who was reaching for his coat at half-time, only for Andy to talk him into giving it ten more minutes, at least. At 3-3, his colleague couldn't have been happier to have been convinced to stay.

Newcastle United-supporting author Aidan Williams watched the final in a Newcastle pub, which was full of students, the demographic offering up a mixture of allegiances but with plenty of Liverpool-sympathising drinkers in attendance, 'It was noisy before kick-off, and very quiet soon after. Several of them left at half-time. True story, I'm afraid. But those that stayed had an incredible time. Raucous second half, disbelieving extra time, and almost inevitable penalty conclusion. Chaotic scenes in the pub at the end. Lots of teenage Scouse students, and indeed non-Scouse Liverpool fans, jumping everywhere, beer flying, carnage. Super stuff.'

Another author, this time the Aston Villa-loving Ivan McDouall, found himself in south-west Wales on the night of the final, 'I was away in Pembrokeshire with a group of teenagers on an outward bound residential. We had no TV in our digs, so all of them were sitting in the minibus listening to it on the radio. Pretty sure the kids nicked off at half-time and snuck some Stella in – so we locked the minibus and never heard the rest!'

Through all of these memories and recollections, the common theme is that Istanbul, and everything that led up to that success, will stay with those who experienced it to their dying day. It is a place and time that is locked within but also has a propensity to spill out at the most random of moments. We were all blessed to be a part of it.

Afterword

LIVERPOOL'S 2004/05 domestic campaign was utterly dysfunctional. Not for one moment were they in the top four of the Premier League, and they were beaten to a Champions League berth by Everton, the first time the Reds had finished lower than their neighbours for 18 years; the first time since Goodison Park had last been the home of the league champions, in 1986/87.

Liverpool won only two times domestically on the weekends that followed the 14 midweek Champions League fixtures that led them to Istanbul.

Within the domestic competitions, Liverpool exited the FA Cup at the first hurdle at Burnley in the strangest of circumstances, this after the game had already been postponed due to a torrential downpour, while in the League Cup there had been a marvellous run to the final, which went against Rafael Benítez's side in cruel circumstances, inclusive of a Steven Gerrard own goal equaliser that came with just 11 minutes remaining of the initial 90. Throughout it all, Liverpool's endeavours in the Champions League sustained them, or at least from the last match of the group stages it did.

Up to that incredible second half against Olympiacos, their European campaign had been just as dysfunctional as their domestic one. Liverpool had contrived to lose at home to the lesser lights of AK Graz in the second leg of the third qualifying round, albeit by a smaller margin than Benítez's side had won in Austria a fortnight earlier. This inauspicious route into the group stage was followed by 495 minutes of Champions League football that flattered to deceive.

Beyond an impressive opening night of Group A, where they comfortably dealt with Monaco at Anfield, over the course of their next four and a half group games none of Benítez's players found the back of the net. Their only goal had been a Jorge Andrade own goal, the sole score at the Estadio Riazor when Liverpool procured a 1-0 victory over Deportivo de La Coruña on matchday four.

What came next in those last 45 minutes against Olympiacos was a tale of the unexpected. Having gone in at half-time trailing to a Rivaldo free kick, Liverpool then proceeded to score the three second-half goals that they needed to preserve their place in the competition. Even then, while Steven Gerrard was the expected all-action hero with the clincher just four minutes from time, the identity of the scorers of their first and second goals that night were totally left-field in origin, as Florent Sinama Pongolle and Neil Mellor would never have been on any Reds supporter's list of likely heroes as the 2004/05 season began.

This wild 45 minutes of football acted as the springboard to a mood swing of biblical proportions, where Liverpool did put a foot wrong occasionally but were always capable of correcting the problem. In the knockout rounds they played seven games, winning five, one via a penalty shoot-out, while drawing two, scoring 12 goals, and keeping three clean sheets. Within this run they conceded six goals, half of those during the first half of the final itself.

Across that same timespan Liverpool also played their last 11 Premier League fixtures of the season. They won only four of them, drawing three and losing four.

Even in the build-up to the knockout stage beginning, from the start of the new year Liverpool had played seven Premier League games prior to the first leg of their last-16 encounter with Bayer Leverkusen, losing four of them, a period in which they had also been knocked out of the FA Cup in comical circumstances.

For Liverpool to go on to become champions of Europe for the fifth time amid this maelstrom of domestic chaos simply made no sense whatsoever, and it was utterly glorious. Nobody saw that success coming. It completely defied footballing gravity. Something magical and surreal was at play.

Celebrations were epic. The journey home had been torturous, and of my travelling party, not one of us had the energy to take to the streets of Liverpool for the homecoming parade given that our flight home had not yet landed as the team's open-top bus set off. But that was all OK. We had been blessed to be in Istanbul, and that the feelings and emotions which we had experienced there could now be shared by those who had watched it on TV screens across the city and surrounding areas was a joy to see. The images were magnificent.

As the dust settled, the summer of 2005 brought fresh drama, new rancour. Once again, Gerrard came close to departing for Chelsea, while in the commercial department supporters were left frustrated that they couldn't get their hands on replica Champions League Cup Final shirts and tracksuit tops, as the fudged lines between the end of Reebok's kit manufacturing contract and the beginning of a reunion with Adidas brought with it chaos in the club shop.

Within 12 months, Benítez's Liverpool had added the FA Cup to their growing honours haul via another dramatic 3-3 draw and penalty shoot-out, this time on a blisteringly hot afternoon in Cardiff against West Ham United, in what would go on to be christened as the 'Gerrard Final'. Another magical day for the memory bank; the future appeared set to be a silver-laden one.

To his squad, Benítez had added Pepe Reina, Daniel Agger, Jan Kronkamp, Mohamed Sissoko, Boudewijn Zenden, and Peter Crouch, while a potential return of Michael Owen, initially on loan from Real Madrid, fell apart after Newcastle United weighed in with a £16.8m bid. Another prodigal son would return in the new year, however, when Robbie Fowler shockingly pulled on a Liverpool shirt once again.

Those successes of 2004/05 and 2005/06 represented glories attained while Liverpool were a team under construction, but they would be denied further honours under Benítez across seasons when they looked much more the finished article: the 2007 Champions League Final went against them in Athens when up against Milan once more, a semi-final defeat followed against Chelsea in 2007/08, and the Premier League title race was lost in 2008/09.

Fernando Torres arrived, and Benítez's team had stepped up a gear, but those near misses on further successes were punishing to the soul, and the dawning of the Tom Hicks and George Gillett era brought with it bluster, showmanship, an unfulfilled new stadium project, broken promises, subterfuge, supporter unions, highly organised and targeted globalised protests, high court drama, and very nearly administration, before John Henry and his colleagues obtained the deeds to the club.

In May 2005, however, all of that was still to come, and all that mattered to Liverpool's supporters was that the glory of Istanbul had turned back the clock a couple of decades, to a time when the club ruled Europe with a confident swagger, a time in history when at the very least with a football at their feet, the world was the city's oyster.

It was an incredible time to be following Liverpool Football Club.